People to Know

Martha Stewart

Successful Businesswoman

Virginia Meachum

Enslow Publishers, Inc.

44 Fadem Road   PO Box 38
Box 699   Aldershot
Springfield, NJ 07081   Hants GU12 6BP
USA   UK

Library of Congress Cataloging-in-Publication Data

Meachum, Virginia.
   Martha Stewart : successful businesswoman / Virginia Meachum.
      p.   cm. — (People to know)
   Includes bibliographical references (p. 99) and index.
   Summary: Details the life and career of the woman whose books and television
shows focus on ways to make the home more interesting.
   ISBN 0-89490-984-3
   1. Stewart, Martha—Juvenile literature. 2. Home economists—United States—
Biography—Juvenile literature. 3. Businesswomen—United States—Biography—
Juvenile literature. [1. Stewart, Martha. 2. Home economists. 3. Businesswomen.
4. Women—Biography.] I. Title. II. Series.
TX140.S74M43 1998
640'.92
[B]—DC21   97-43578
                                                                      CIP
                                                                       AC

Printed in the United States of America

10 9 8 7 6 5 4 3 2 1

Illustration Credits:
AP/Wide World Photos, p. 39; Barnard College Archives, p. 21; Courtesy of
Nutley High School, p. 16; Ed Geller/Globe Photos, Inc., p. 87; Edward S.
Sant, p. 53; Everett Collection, p. 4; Fitzroy Barrett/Globe Photos, Inc., p.
55; Harry Benson, p. 34; James M. Kelly/Globe Photos, Inc., p. 76; Jerry
Simpson/Everett Collection, p. 45; Matthew Jordan Smith/Everett
Collection, p. 63, 65; Matthew Jordan Smith/Visages, p. 79; Robert
Roche/Everett Collection, p. 31; Tim Roske AP/Wide World Photos, p. 91;
Walter Weissman/Globe Photos, Inc., p. 71.

Cover Illustration: Matthew Jordan Smith/Visages

Contents

Martha Stewart

A Good Thing

In this age of fast food and overscheduled lives, the media are buzzing over the fact that one woman—with a passion for fine cooking and creativity—has invaded millions of homes across the nation. She is Martha Stewart, known for her skill and style in cooking, decorating, gardening, and home entertaining. Her mission is to make everyday life at home more attractive—that is, more pleasing to the eye, satisfying to the palate, and warmly comfortable for family and friends.

While learning how to share her homekeeping expertise with a wide audience, she also developed expertise in another area—the world of business:

Martha Stewart became an outstanding business-woman.

What is so captivating about this sudden icon of the press and television? Larry King on CNN calls her "America's Hostess."[1] *Esquire* magazine lists her among "Women We Love."[2] *New York* magazine writes of her as "the definitive American woman of our time."[3]

Martha Stewart offers viewers her vision of what America has always been based upon—home and family. She gives it to them in a way that inspires their creative spirits. In bringing her easy-to-follow ideas to the public through every form of media, she convinces legions of fans that they, too, can do as she does. They, too, can enhance their lifestyle and that of their families.

First it was books. In 1982 her first published book, *Entertaining*, a full-color cookbook, was an immediate best-seller. The next year she wrote *Martha Stewart's Quick Cook: 200 Easy and Elegant Recipes*. More books followed on weddings, Christmas, gardening, decorating, and other topics. By 1997, more than five million copies of Stewart's lifestyle books were in print.

Then came *Martha Stewart Living* television. On a daily, half-hour show, this tall, slim woman, who was once a professional model, presents three or more cooking, gardening, or home-improvement projects for her viewers to learn about.

Slowly, clearly, she demonstrates and explains each step. In her reassuring, husky voice, Martha, as she is popularly known, might demonstrate how to plant a peony garden, bake a fresh ham in grass (six-inch-long, organically grown grass), or decorate a lamb cake for Easter. When finished, she will most likely say, "It's a good thing." Each day, an estimated five million viewers tune in to watch Stewart's presentation and be inspired to share in this "good thing."

Browsing the local newsstand, you will find this lifestyle advisor there, too—often pictured on the cover of *Martha Stewart Living*. This magazine is filled with ideas that once again appeal to the reader's creative spirit. Half a million copies are sold each month.

The Martha By Mail service was introduced in the June 1996 issue of *Martha Stewart Living*. Martha By Mail offers kits, gifts, and tools for the home, the garden, and for "just plain living." The products enable a TV viewer or magazine reader to make a project that has been demonstrated. In line with Stewart's philosophy of "inspiration, information, and creation," the products are designed to turn "dreamers into doers."[4] A stationery kit, for example, provides all of the material needed to emboss (decorate with a raised design) and monogram letter-writing paper. The complete kit includes twenty sheets of paper, ten heavyweight note cards, with matching envelopes for each, the embosser, and embosser disks for three designs, including one with the purchaser's initials.

For readers or viewers with questions, the "Ask Martha" column, syndicated by *The New York Times*, appears in more than 160 newspapers across America. A variety of questions, such as which plants to choose for a window box, how to convert an old oil lamp to electric power, or how to make chocolate sorbet, are all answered in the "Ask Martha" column. And Martha Stewart is just warming up. Her presence promises to become even more widespread. On February 5, 1997, the following headline appeared in *The Wall Street Journal*: "Martha Stewart Takes Over Control of Her Empire in Split with Time, Inc."[5] After months of negotiation, Martha Stewart officially gained control of her own company. Naming it Martha Stewart Living Omnimedia, Stewart became its chief executive officer (CEO).

In September 1997, the new company launched three more projects: *Martha Stewart Living*, a daily television show on CBS, replacing Stewart's former syndicated program of the same name; *Ask Martha*, a daily national radio show; and a World Wide Web site (www.marthastewart.com) offering a program guide for the TV show and related information. For Martha Stewart, these major, wide-reaching projects must truly be a "good thing."

Stewart also does a weekly televised how-to segment on CBS-TV's *This Morning*. She makes guest appearances on such television talk shows as *Larry King Live, Charlie Rose,* and *The David Letterman Show.* She also travels from coast to coast doing lectures and book signings.

How does Martha Stewart fit it all in? And how did a young woman from a modest, Polish-American family in New Jersey manage to build a multimedia empire?

A Head Start

Home and family would unknowingly lead Martha Stewart to her present-day celebrity. Born on August 3, 1941, in Jersey City, New Jersey, Martha was the second child of Edward and Martha (Ruszkowski) Kostyra.

Edward Kostyra, the son of Polish immigrants, was a strong, athletic, physical-education teacher. He left his low-paying teaching job, however, to work as a pharmaceutical salesman to better support his growing family. His wife, Martha, was also a teacher, but she devoted herself full-time to homemaking while their family was young. She would return to elementary-level teaching after the youngest child was in school.

When Martha was about three years old, the Kostyras moved from an apartment in Jersey City to a house on Elm Place in Nutley, New Jersey. Nutley is a suburban, working-class community not far from New York City. In their modest two-story, three-bedroom house, the Kostyras would raise their family, which grew to include six children. Eric was the oldest. Then came Martha, three years younger, followed by Frank, Kathy, George, and Laura.

The Kostyras were a home-centered family. With only one income, they had no money for such luxuries as expensive toys, vacations, or dining out. As the children were growing up, they all had household chores to do, and for recreation the center of their activity was the kitchen table. Here they gathered to play card games or Scrabble and to listen to the radio—but only if they had finished their schoolwork. Some of the popular radio programs at that time were *Ozzie and Harriet*, *The Shadow*, and *The Lone Ranger*.

Edward Kostyra went into New York City every day to work, and he often brought home unusual fruit from city markets for his children. Fruits such as pomegranates, persimmons, and pineapples were a special treat in the 1940s and 1950s, and Martha learned early to enjoy the taste and texture of out-of-the-ordinary foods.

As the oldest girl in the family, Martha was taught many home-related skills. From her father, an avid gardener, she learned about designing, planting, and caring for a garden. On their long, sloping backyard (only fifty feet wide), Edward Kostyra worked laboriously, digging earth and laying rocks to create an upper terrace for a vegetable garden and a lower terrace for fruit trees and flowers. During the winter months, father and daughter spent long evenings studying garden catalogs, planning the summer garden, and ordering seeds. When the seeds arrived, he taught Martha how to start tomatoes, green peppers, and other vegetables indoors. Together they planted the seeds in the bottoms of milk cartons filled with special soil made from peat moss, vermiculite, and sand. After the seeds began to sprout, Martha and her father kept dozens of seedlings warm and watered in the family kitchen until the outdoor planting season arrived. A large, vacant field behind the Kostyras' yard, part of an unused farm, provided extra room for growing more vegetables.

Martha was the only one of her father's children who shared his passion for gardening. He was an exacting teacher, "a total perfectionist," noted Martha.[1] But she was receptive to that kind of teaching. She never minded spending hours weeding and planting on a hot summer day.[2] In recalling those childhood summers, Martha wrote, "Although not yet in high school, I knew then that I wanted my own garden, one where I could express myself and grow my own things."[3]

Edward Kostyra also taught his daughter about flower arranging. He planted many varieties of flowers and kept the house supplied with fresh-picked blooms. He taught Martha about selecting the right container and arranging the flowers by color and form. One summer, she put together a bouquet of pansies, roses, and peony buds in one of her mother's old teapots and entered it in a local flower show. The small arrangement won a blue ribbon.

From her mother, Martha learned about cooking, baking, and sewing. At age eight, she was given a cookbook with easy-to-follow recipes that were suitable for a child. Martha Kostyra encouraged her young daughter to try out some of the recipes and turned her loose in the kitchen. By following the simple directions, which were illustrated with drawings, the would-be cook had soon tried them all. Her favorite recipe was for butterscotch candy, which she reported "was better than any store-bought butterscotch."[4]

Martha Kostyra, like her husband, was of Polish descent, and much of her cooking was adapted from European family-style recipes. A savory mushroom soup made with large Polish mushrooms, and pierogi—tasty dumplings stuffed with a sweet cabbage filling—were two traditional dishes that young Martha learned to make. Her grandmother Franciska Ruszkowski also added to her cooking experience. On summer visits to her grandmother's home in Buffalo, New York, Martha helped pick cherries, peaches, strawberries, and whatever other fruit was in season. Then she learned about preserving fruits to make jams and jellies. She also watched her grandmother prepare unusual dishes, like carp stuffed with fish mousse.

Other relatives had special food skills, too. Martha's Uncle Joe in Jersey City was a butcher, and she learned about various cuts of meat from watching him work. Her Aunt Mary specialized in making salads. Another uncle ran a delicatessen, for which his wife made Polish sausage every day.

Martha's culinary ventures stretched beyond her mother's kitchen to the house of Mr. and Mrs. Maus, German bakers who lived next door. Although retired, they continued to turn out breads, rolls, and coffee cakes almost daily, filling the neighborhood with a tempting fragrance. The Mauses often welcomed Martha, along with her brothers and sisters, into their basement kitchen. Here the children watched huge bowls of risen dough being shaped into loaves, placed on metal sheets to rise again, and then baked in vast commercial-style gas ovens. The young Kostyras were invited to sample the oven-fresh bread as well as tasty cakes and strudels.

Martha returned often to the Maus kitchen and helped as a flour sifter and a taster. Later, she was taught the art of kneading dough and other bread-making skills. Eventually, in her mother's kitchen, she experimented with making a variety of breads— white, whole wheat, raisin. It was a skill that would serve her well in the years to come. The Mauses also taught Martha to make cherry pie and peach tarts, using fruit from the Montmorency cherry tree and the white-peach tree that grew in their backyard. She was already familiar with that peach tree. Often she would climb up with a book and pillow and spend many summer hours reading in the boughs. As she grew older, the novels of Edith Wharton, the romantic classics of Sir Walter Scott, and Leo Tolstoy's *Anna Karenina* were among her reading choices.

Despite a tight budget for a family of eight, food

was plentiful in the Kostyra kitchen. During the growing season, their large garden provided a healthful variety of fresh vegetables, berries, and other fruit for daily meals. Any surplus that was harvested would be canned and stored for winter use. Occasionally, Martha's father would go fishing and return with an abundance of fish as well as hard-shell crabs. Sometimes on a Saturday morning, Martha and her brother Eric bicycled to their favorite trout stream to fish for speckled trout. Their mother would serve it grilled or sautéed for supper that night.

By the age of ten, Martha was channeling some of her energy into baby-sitting for fifty cents an hour. She discovered that if she did "extra-special things," she would get paid more. So she began to organize birthday parties for children in the neighborhood, thus adding to her earnings.[5]

Martha was only thirteen when a friend encouraged her to try out at a New York modeling agency. Before long, her blond hair and good looks brought part-time modeling assignments in television commercials for Clairol hair products and Lifebuoy soap. On Saturdays, she modeled high-fashion dresses at the Bonwit Teller department store in New York City.

Meanwhile, at home, Martha was about to experience another phase of homemaking—that of remodeling. When the Kostyras moved to Elm Place in 1944, the original kitchen was adequate for a family of four. By 1955, the larger family needed more space in this activity-centered room. They decided to remodel. Keeping in mind their limited budget, Ed Kostyra drew up a new floor plan, eliminating the pantry in favor of new kitchen cabinets.

Martha was put in charge of demolition, which meant knocking down an interior wall to open up more space. The whole family voted on the color choice for the countertop, linoleum floor, and large oval table and chairs. They chose pink. Later they would look upon this color as "a grave error"—it was overpowering in such a large space.[6] That was another learning experience.

Throughout her grade school and high school years, Martha was a dedicated student, so much so that she was often known as "the teacher's pet." But that didn't seem to bother her. "If you're working by the teacher's side," she told PBS-TV talk-show host Charlie Rose, "you are going to learn more than anybody else."[7] She cared about her teachers, often inviting them home for lunch or dinner. "And," she continued, "the table was always big enough for whoever we wanted to bring home. . . . That was a nice thing about our family. . . . There was always room. . . . There was always enough food."[8]

Edward and Martha Kostyra were industrious, caring parents who encouraged their children in many ways. "We were brought up unpretentiously but with a lot of spirit and a lot of 'You can do anything you want to do' hammered into our heads," Martha has said. "We were given the idea of limitless opportunity. It was a wonderful way to grow up."[9]

As a student at Nutley High School, Martha was an eager learner, ambitious, and always ready to tackle a new project. One of her projects was to prepare a

Nutley High School in 1959, the year Martha Kostyra graduated.

large breakfast for the entire high school football team. This could have been an intimidating challenge, but coming from a family of eight, Martha understood about cooking in large quantities. When the project was accomplished, it became her first catering experience.

Martha continued to work part-time as a model, also actively participating in school activities and keeping up her rating as an A student. Martha graduated from Nutley High School in 1959.

Moving On

In the fall of 1959, Martha Kostyra enrolled at Barnard College in New York City, where she had been offered a partial scholarship. She would live at home in New Jersey and commute to the campus. Nutley is thirteen miles from New York City. Her modeling jobs would help pay for her education.[1]

Why did she choose Barnard? "The smallness of the college, and the ability to be within a big university and yet be in an independent college" appealed to her, she said.[2] Barnard College, an independent liberal arts college for women, is part of Columbia University.

The enrollment at Barnard consists of students from all over the United States and from more than forty countries. Among the many graduates who have achieved distinction in their work are anthropologist Margaret Mead; Jeane Kirkpatrick, former U.S. ambassador to the United Nations; Anna Quindlen, Pulitzer Prize–winning columnist for *The New York Times*; Twyla Tharp, choreographer and dancer; and author Hortense Calisher.[3]

At Barnard, Kostyra concentrated on studying art, European history, and architectural history. "Architecture was one of my great loves. It still is," she explained later. "And art history and history was another great interest. So that's why I put them together."[4]

Following that first semester of commuting from home, Kostyra accepted a job through the placement office at Barnard. She became the live-in cook for two elderly sisters who lived in a twelve-room apartment on upper Fifth Avenue. She cooked breakfast and dinner in return for a room in the servants' quarters. This enabled her to live closer to the campus.

Blond, tall (five feet nine inches), and attractive, Kostyra continued to accept modeling assignments to help with her college expenses. One assignment was a brief trip to Paris to model spring clothes. During her sophomore year, she was named one of *Glamour* magazine's "Ten Best Dressed College Girls of 1961."[5]

Martha had a fully packed schedule—attending classes, studying, and working—but she did manage some time for social activities. In the library one day, near the end of Kostyra's freshman year, a classmate pulled out a photo of her brother, Andrew Stewart. He was a law student at Yale University. She offered to set up a date for him and Kostyra to meet.

When Andrew Stewart (known as Andy) met Martha Kostyra, he said, "I immediately fell in love."[6] In the spring of Kostyra's sophomore year, they became engaged. A few months later, they made plans to get married. Andy's mother did not approve of their decision because of Kostyra's young age. She was nineteen. Her father also disapproved and told his daughter she was crazy.[7] But Kostyra was determined to go ahead with the plan anyway "because Andy was honest and extremely serious. Until then, my boyfriends had been fun-seekers."[8]

The bride-to-be worked thoughtfully to arrange a wedding within the limited means of her parents. Unforeseen at that time were the elaborate weddings she would one day plan as a well-known bridal consultant. With help from her mother, Martha made her own bridal dress—a white organdy gown with embroidered daisies. Andy's mother provided daisy flowers for the bouquets. The wedding was small, with only the immediate families and closest friends invited to St. Paul's Chapel on the campus of Columbia University.

On July 1, 1961, to the sound of organ music chosen by Andy, and with her sister Kathy (age fifteen) as maid of honor, Martha Kostyra became Martha Stewart. The ceremony was followed by a simple luncheon, including wedding cake, in the Barberry Room of the Berkshire Hotel in New York City. To keep expenses down, no professional photographer was present to record this joyful occasion. Only a few snapshots were taken. But memory would serve the bride well. Almost thirty-five years later, describing her wedding day in a "Remembering" column in *Martha Stewart Living* magazine, Martha wrote, "In my mind . . . I have an absolutely clear image of every moment, formal and informal, each one full of joy and happiness."[9]

That fall, the newlyweds settled in Connecticut near Yale so that Andy could continue his law school studies. They shared a rented house with another student couple. Martha Stewart agreed to delay returning to Barnard for her junior year. Meanwhile, she accepted modeling assignments in New York to provide the income they needed.

In June 1962, Stewart graduated from Yale Law School and they moved to a small, inexpensive apartment near the Columbia University campus in New York City. Martha Stewart returned to Barnard and immersed herself in making up the courses she had missed. She also continued working as a model. Andy did research part-time for a law firm and studied for a master of laws degree at Columbia University's law school.

Two years later, in 1964, Martha Stewart graduated from Barnard College with a bachelor of arts degree in European history and architecture. That same year, Andy completed his graduate work at Columbia. To reward themselves, the Stewarts went to Europe for a delayed honeymoon.

In addition to the excitement of traveling through foreign countries, they experienced many new foods in the cafés, restaurants, and dining rooms of Italy,

Martha Stewart graduated from Barnard College in 1964, with a degree in European history and architecture. Pictured here is Milbank Hall on the Barnard campus in the 1960s.

France, and Germany. Martha Stewart's attention was also drawn to the presentation of food—the appealing way it was arranged on the plate—even the way the napkins were folded. She made mental notes of all these things. She asked questions of chefs at every opportunity.[10]

Upon returning to New York, Andy Stewart joined a New York law firm and Martha Stewart worked full-time as a model. They improved their living quarters by moving into a spacious apartment on Riverside Drive overlooking the Hudson River. To furnish the six rooms, they hunted for furniture at auctions, flea markets, and antique shops. This opened up another area of interest for Martha. In shopping around, she learned a great deal about furniture design, quality, restoration, and the art of bargaining. Early in 1965, she and Andy also learned that one of their six rooms would be needed for a nursery. Martha Stewart was pregnant. Their baby was due to arrive in the fall. For the next several months, the Stewarts spent many hours together remodeling, redecorating, and fur-nishing a room to welcome their child.

Despite living in the city, Martha was attracted, as in her childhood, to nature and gardening. On week-ends, she and Andy would drive throughout the Northeast countryside, watching for early-blooming trees and flowering shrubs. She was particularly fond of lilacs, which had been common around her child-hood home. Whenever they were available, she would gather armloads of the colorful blooms—purple, blue, magenta—and fill the apartment with huge, scented arrangements. Unable to resist the lure of gardening, she grew herb plants in the kitchen and raised orchids in the bathtub as she awaited the birth of their baby.

Daughter Alexis was born on September 27, 1965. When she was a month old, the Stewarts bought an 1890 one-room schoolhouse on fifty acres of woodland in Middlefield, Massachusetts. This weekend retreat in the Berkshire Mountains would give them a place where they both could garden, and Alexis could thrive in the pure country air. But with no plumbing, and only a fireplace for heat and a potbellied stove for cooking, the lifestyle was primitive. Martha and Andy took turns carrying water from a mountain stream half a mile away to supply their needs. With young Alexis by her side, Martha gardened, Andy chopped wood for the fireplace, and together they gathered mushrooms, wild strawberries, and blueberries — making the most of their back-to-nature weekends.

For the next five years, they spent weekends and summers in Middlefield, improving the house, painting, decorating, and growing such an abundance of vegetables that they had plenty to share with their friends in both New York and Middlefield. In August of their first growing season, Martha Stewart entered some of her produce in the county fair at Middlefield. Her cabbages, cauliflowers, and tomatoes all won ribbons, and it pleased her to be "a participant in the farming community."[11]

While Middlefield satisfied Stewart's love of gardening, her love of cooking was fulfilled by entertaining friends in their city apartment. The first Christmas in their Riverside Drive apartment, they had an open house party, inviting everyone they knew. As Stewart described it, "I spent many happy weeks planning and preparing for that party, with our three-month-old daughter Alexis watching and 'helping' from her baby chair in the kitchen."[12] A vast variety of food was served during the evening party, along with eggnog and many kinds of Christmas cookies. The Stewarts' party was such a success, it became an annual tradition for them.

In the fall of 1967, when Alexis was two years old, Martha Stewart thought about getting a job. She had studied economics, and the investment process intrigued her. She and Andy had invested their wedding present money in the stock market. Confident that Alexis would be in the care of good help at home, Stewart joined a young Wall Street firm as a stockbroker.

She worked hard and learned a lot about basic business—what made money and what didn't. As the nation's economy climbed, so did her income. By the early seventies, Martha Stewart was earning more than $100,000 a year.[13] The work was exciting but demanded full-time involvement. She started at the office early in the morning and often worked with clients until late at night. This left little time for family life as she had known it while growing up in Nutley, New Jersey. When the stock market slowed in 1973, Stewart's job became less profitable, and she decided to leave the brokerage firm. She wanted to spend more time with her daughter, and she was ready to turn her attention to more home-centered activities.

A New Direction

The year before she left the brokerage firm, Stewart and her husband had purchased an abandoned farmhouse in Westport, Connecticut. Built in 1805, the house at Turkey Hill had been so neglected that it was considered the "Westport Horror" by local residents.[1] The Stewarts had planned to fix it up and sell it. But now that Martha Stewart was no longer working on Wall Street, she and Andy decided to move to Connecticut and renovate the house while living in it.

The Stewarts moved to Westport in 1973. During the week, while Andy commuted daily to his work in New York City as a corporate lawyer, Martha Stewart stayed at home, caring for Alexis, gardening, cooking, and painting the house—inside and out. Over the next two years, using what they had learned from remodeling their Middlefield schoolhouse and from talking with local experts, the Stewarts completely renovated the farmhouse. Working at night and on weekends, they tore down walls, installed windows, added bathrooms and cabinets, restored the seven fireplaces to usable condition, and made numerous other improvements.

Meanwhile, they had an opportunity to buy four acres of adjoining property, giving them a total of six acres. The added land was quickly put into production. They had already started an orchard, planting forty-five fruit trees before ever moving into the house. Among them were apple, sour cherry, and white peach—familiar trees from Martha Stewart's childhood and a future source of fruit for making the pies, tarts, and jellies she remembered. From a nearby nursery they added quince, pear, and plum trees. Edward Kostyra, who had come to help with the gardening, planted a fig tree for them just like the one his daughter had known while growing up on Elm Place in Nutley, New Jersey.

Half an acre was turned into a garden bearing a wide variety of vegetables, herbs, currants, and blueberries—the berry bushes having been transported from the Middlefield property. The Stewarts developed a flower garden, added a second barn, a henhouse, and two beehives, each containing about eighty thousand bees. They acquired chickens, turkeys, geese, two baby goats, and one black sheep. Alexis fed the goats warm milk from baby bottles.

It was Martha Stewart's plan to have Alexis learn to care for and love as many animals as they could manage. She strongly believed that caring for pets and helping with chickens and barnyard animals would teach children the importance of work, responsibility, and friendship.

There were also household pets—a growing assortment of adopted cats, ranging from gray-striped tabby to exotic Blue Persian and Himalayan, and a pair of chow dogs. (A chow, or chow chow, is a Chinese breed of dog with a thick collar of fur around its neck, and a blue-black tongue.) At one time, the feline residents totaled nine—all of them bathed and groomed every Saturday by their mistress.

For Martha Stewart, the move to Westport would influence the rest of her life. "That was the first inkling I had, I think," she told PBS-TV talk-show host Charlie Rose, "that making a home, raising a family was more important to me than anything else. . . . I decided then and there that the home was really my place. I really loved it. I loved the garden. I loved decorating, designing, cooking."[2]

After major remodeling of the house at Turkey Hill had been completed, and the garden and orchard were in place, Martha Stewart decided to learn more about the art of cooking. She had first become interested in gourmet cooking—preparing fine and exotic food—on her brief trip to Europe for a modeling assignment while at Barnard. After her marriage to Andy and their first trip together through Europe, she sometimes accompanied him on business trips abroad. No matter what foreign city they were in, local food and its preparation always caught her interest.

During Martha Stewart's years as a stockbroker, she often took business clients to lunch or dinner as part of her job. Dining in some of New York City's finest restaurants, she would order an unusual entrée, vegetable, or salad. Then she would try to discover what made it unique. Sometimes she would ask the chef about the ingredients and then try to create a similar dish in her apartment kitchen.

In her Westport kitchen, with a copy of Julia Child's *Mastering the Art of French Cooking* as her guide, Martha Stewart studiously worked at trying out every recipe in the book. Julia Child taught Americans that home cooking could be fine cuisine. Her 1961 cookbook is still considered a classic.

By now, Stewart missed being around other people, so she decided to give cooking lessons in her kitchen. She started with children about the age of Alexis—seven and eight years old. "I gave them chef's hats and they learned to cook omelets," Stewart recalls. "Everyone had a good time—including me."[3] Then she went on to conduct cooking classes for adults. Although she had no formal training as a chef and had never worked in a restaurant, Stewart had an enthusiasm for cooking and a natural talent for creating new ways to present food.

In 1976, Stewart rented space in Westport and opened a take-out gourmet food shop called the Market Basket. She installed a professional stove and refrigerator and designed a workspace for herself. She organized a group of local women to produce baked goods and other fresh food for sale in the shop, along with her own food products. The sales were excellent, but a year later more space was needed. Rather than move to a larger facility, Stewart decided to run a catering business from her home.

The Market Basket had brought her to the attention of other women in the community who were interested in starting their own food businesses. Based on her experience, Stewart offered several tips: Inquire into local health laws about using your kitchen for a commercial purpose. Find out about insurance: what type and how much you will need. Ask a local newspaper to do a story on your shop.[4]

To provide home workspace for the catering business, the Stewarts converted a section of their basement into a kitchen. They furnished it with the stove, refrigerator, and other equipment from the Market Basket. When Martha Stewart placed an ad in the local paper offering her service as a caterer, people responded immediately. Her first big-party request was to prepare the food and serve a wedding buffet for three hundred guests. Inexperience led her to choose a menu that was overly elaborate for a beginning caterer.

On that 103-degree afternoon in August, under a breezeless tent at a Long Island Sound beach club, the gelatin quickly melted around the *oeufs en gelée* (eggs in gelatin), and the top layer of the elaborate wedding cake began to slide sideways. Stewart immediately removed the eggs from the buffet table, nudged the cake layer back in place, and continued serving the guests. No one else seemed aware of the problems.

The whole affair was a learning experience for the novice caterer. She learned that for a successful party, the hostess must work hard to avoid disasters. She also learned, and later wrote, "No one will know about your disasters if you don't tell him."[5]

Requests for her catering services were so numerous that Stewart decided to go into a partnership with her friend Norma Collier. Their catering business, called "The Uncatered Affair," was highly successful, but it was not without stress. Within the year they ended the partnership. In a later interview, Collier said that she did not wish to work "128 hours a week" and that she chose to return to "a more balanced life."[6]

Stewart continued the business from her Turkey Hill kitchen, catering to such notable Connecticut neighbors as opera singer Beverly Sills, actor Robert Redford and his wife, and Joanne Woodward and Paul Newman of Hollywood fame. Each one had special catering requests. Beverly Sills liked the chocolate Victoria tartlets. The Redfords liked zucchini and banana bread. The Newmans ordered chicken teriyaki to serve to Paul's car-racing crew.[7]

Stewart created a new company called Martha Stewart, Inc., and extended her service to all types of social events. She continued to teach a weekly cooking class. As she became more knowledgeable about food and entertaining, she began contributing articles to *The New York Times* and *Family Circle* magazine. Stewart also wrote a "Quick Cook" column for *House*

Early in her catering business, Martha Stewart did the cooking and baking in her Turkey Hill Farm kitchen. She is shown here with a squash pie, garnished with leaves cut from pastry scraps and baked until golden brown.

Beautiful. In June 1977, the Stewarts' Turkey Hill Farm was featured as "the good life, country style" in *House and Garden* magazine. Included were Martha Stewart's recipes, photographs of a hall mural and a floor, both handpainted by Stewart, and her instructions for stenciling a floor. How did she feel about these challenges? "The thing is not to feel anything is unconquerable," she said.[8]

Stewart's business had now outgrown its basement kitchen. Early in 1981, she moved the operation into a building next to the house, gaining a larger kitchen, with more equipment and counter space. Here, her three assistant cooks and other staff members could more efficiently prepare the hors d'oeuvres (appetizers), salads, entrées, and desserts requested by her numerous clients. To acquire the many waiters and waitresses needed for her parties, Stewart hired students from her Westport neighborhood as well as young actors and actresses in New York who welcomed temporary employment.

What does a caterer need to know to produce a successful party? First, a meeting must take place between the client (the person giving the party) and the caterer (the person in charge of producing the party). At this meeting, the caterer requests such basic information as the date of the event, the occasion (birthday, wedding, graduation party, etc.), and where the event is to be held. This could be in the client's home, a private club, office, gymnasium, or any other suitable place. The caterer also needs to know the number of guests and whether this is to be a morning, midday, or evening gathering. A budget—the amount the client wishes to spend on the party—must also be discussed. Menus may be suggested by either the client or the caterer or both. When they have agreed upon the plans, a contract between the two parties is then signed. The caterer is now in charge of the event.

In Martha Stewart's business, her staff prepared the food, using her own recipes. They often used fresh vegetables, herbs, and fruit from her garden. To ensure a smooth-running party, arrangements were made well in advance for kitchen assistants, bartenders, waiters, and waitresses. Also, one person was in charge of the kitchen area, and another in charge of the serving staff on the day of the affair.

Stewart's business continued to grow at an incredible rate. She was now catering parties ranging in size from intimate dinners for twelve people to business receptions for a thousand guests. Stewart never seemed intimidated by extremely big parties, which, because of their long guest lists, would have to be held in large places, often without kitchen conveniences. No matter—Stewart and her staff would bring with them whatever equipment was needed.

At one catered affair, Stewart prepared and served hors d'oeuvres for two hundred patrons of the Museum of American Folk Art. Despite the setting—a vast, barren armory in New York City with no kitchen—the enormous quantity of food needed was prepared in advance, the serving was carefully organized, and the event ran smoothly. "Everything she does is exceptional," said the programs manager of the Cooper-Hewitt National Design Museum in New

A view of the restored 1805 farmhouse at Turkey Hill. In the building at the left is the roomy studio kitchen, which was needed for Stewart's growing catering business. Martha Stewart sits in the foreground with her daughter's dog.

York City.[9] Stewart catered about four big parties a year at that museum.

Other unusual party settings have been the American courtyard of the Metropolitan Museum of Art, the promenade in Lincoln Center, and even the rotunda of the once-empty United States Customs House in New York City. Some of her parties revolved around themes, such as a Victorian country fair, a Mexican fiesta, a Moroccan dinner party.

In speaking about her decision to concentrate on her catering business, Stewart later said, "Nothing is more difficult . . . I did it out of my home. . . . but I still was able to develop and create a business. That turned out to be the basis for everything else I was going to do."[10]

During the time that Martha Stewart was concentrating on her growing business, her husband had been meeting new demands in his career. Andrew Stewart focused his legal expertise on the publishing business. In 1976, he advanced from his position as executive vice-president of Harry N. Abrams, Inc., to become president of the company. Abrams published large, prestigious art books such as *Chagall by Chagall.*

In 1980, the Stewarts attended a party at the Cooper-Hewitt Museum, catered by Martha Stewart. Here, she met Alan Mirken, who was then the president of Crown Publishers. He was interested in her catering work and invited her to produce a book for Clarkson N. Potter, Inc., the lifestyle division of the Crown Publishing Group.

For some time, Stewart had been thinking about writing a book based on her catering experiences. She accepted Mirken's offer, and another venture was about to begin.

The Good
and the Bad

With her catering business firmly established, Stewart was ready to take on a book project. In the fall of 1980, she signed a contract with Clarkson N. Potter, Inc., to write a book on entertaining. Her vision for the book was far different from the standard cookbook, which was usually limited to recipes and methods of cooking. Although Stewart's book would present recipes, the emphasis would be on all aspects of entertaining at home—on sharing the home with family and friends.

In the planning stage, her publishers thought her ideas were good and went along with almost every-thing. At that time, most photographs in cookbooks were in black and white. Stewart wanted color. The publishers were doubtful. They suggested half in color and half in black and white. Stewart remained firm, finally convincing them, she said, "that food really looked better in color."[1] The publisher then suggested that the size of the proposed book be reduced by half. The discussion went on in meeting after meeting, but Stewart's vision of a large-size, coffee-table book eventually won out.[2]

For the next two years, along with catering and meeting other demands in her daily life, Stewart worked on the book. Much would be based on what she had learned through her past experience in creating unique menus and planning successful parties. "Without the catering business," she said, "I could never have written this book."[3]

Much energy and time go into the production of a book as detailed and elaborate as the one planned by Stewart. A longtime friend, Elizabeth Hawes, worked with her on the text. Another friend, Michael Skott, worked long hours on preparing photographs for the book, and Roger Black planned the overall design.

In 1982, *Entertaining*, the first full-color cookbook/entertaining book ever written, was ready to make its appearance. Martha Stewart's dedication of the book read "To Andy, my husband, for his encouragement, good nature, and support. Alexis, my daughter, for her patience. My father, for instilling in me a love for all things beautiful."

The first printing of *Entertaining*—twenty-five thousand copies—sold out quickly. To meet the demand, other printings followed, year after year. By 1998, the book would be in its thirtieth printing.[4]

The three-hundred-page, oversize, elegantly illustrated book features ideas on home entertaining from simple to elaborate, Written in a graceful, flowing style, Stewart's book is filled with personal anecdotes and suggestions for thirty-five types of parties, along with easy-to-follow recipes and decorating ideas. Color photographs illustrate the imaginative table settings and ready-to-serve food.

The book's party ideas include "A Sunday Omelette Brunch" with three choices of omelette, and a "Kitchen Salad Party" featuring nine varieties of salad, homemade carrot and zucchini breads, and French baguettes (long, narrow loaves). All are shown served with tempting desserts.

Stewart also includes some favorite family recipes, like her mother's mushroom soup, her grandmother's marbleized hard-boiled eggs, and daughter Alexis's Brown Sugar Chocolate Chip Cookies. For the courageous in a holiday spirit, there are directions for making a gingerbread mansion, and for the occasion of an at-home wedding, a step-by-step guide tells how to create a five-tier wedding cake garnished with pink hyacinth blossoms and glossy leaves.

Martha Stewart's *Entertaining* brought favorable reviews. Noted one reviewer about the author, "She sees entertaining as an opportunity to express warmth, individuality, and personal taste, not as a requirement to redecorate the home."[5] Another wrote that the author has "a fine eye, a sense of theater, and a respect for both the physical beauty and the taste of food."[6]

The idea of serving creative, attractive food as a

Martha Stewart and Ruth Leserman, a San Francisco restaurant consultant, chop mushrooms in preparation for a luncheon to celebrate the 1982 publication of Stewart's first book, Entertaining.

way of entertaining stirred the imagination of readers. Martha Stewart's multicity tour—to meet people, promote the book, and autograph copies—brought her recognition from coast to coast.

This was only the beginning of her book projects. She had many more ideas to share. The following year, 1983, Crown Publishers released her second book, *Martha Stewart's Quick Cook: 200 Easy and Elegant Recipes*. The dedication reads: "To my mother, Martha Kostyra, and her mother, my early teachers." This book, too, was favorably received. The book contained plans for three-course and four-course meals that could be prepared in less than one hour. Although some reviewers doubted this could be accomplished by anyone but Stewart, a book critic for *Library Journal* found *Martha Stewart's Quick Cook* to have "dash, charm, ease, and elegance."[7]

Stewart continued to operate the catering business as well as to produce more books: *Martha Stewart's Hors d'Oeuvres: The Creation and Presentation of Fabulous Finger Foods* (1984), and *Martha Stewart's Pies and Tarts* (1985).

Each new publication brought another book tour and a growing number of Martha Stewart fans. She was now in popular demand to give demonstrations, lectures, and cooking seminars and to speak at charity luncheons and dinners. *Time* magazine called her "the guru of good taste (and taste buds) in American entertaining, looked to by millions of American women for guidance about everything from weddings to weeding."[8]

Although Stewart had a vast number of admirers, she also had a number of detractors—people who found fault with her or with her work. This first became evident in 1982 after the publication of *Entertaining*. Some members of the food establishment accused Stewart of plagiarism (copying someone's work—in this case recipes—without giving proper credit). *Newsweek* reported that her orange almond cake and a cherry pound cake with raisins had appeared earlier in Julia Child's *Mastering the Art of French Cooking*. Barbara Tropp, author of *The*

Modern Art of Chinese Cooking, complained that several of her own recipes were featured in *Entertaining*, although she took no formal legal action against Stewart.[9]

A charge of plagiarism is not easy to prove in the case of recipes. By making only minor changes, a recipe can easily be made "new." Stewart said that she had developed her recipes during her many years in the catering business. The controversy eventually died down. In future books, however, Stewart indicated the source of a recipe whenever appropriate.

In addition to books, Stewart began to produce seminars at her headquarters in Westport, Connecticut. Enthusiastic fans, women and men from all over the United States, signed up a year in advance, and paid $900 to $1,200, to attend one of her three- or four-day Entertaining Seminars. A group of twenty to thirty participants attended morning and afternoon sessions in the immaculate, stainless-steel kitchen at Martha Stewart's Westport office. After a breakfast of hot coffee and tea, along with lemon scones, or sticky buns, or perhaps orange French toast, the participants settled onto folding chairs to watch Stewart prepare such dishes as Smoked Trout Mousse, Oriental Five-Spice Hen with Curried Couscous Stuffing, or Green Tomato Mincemeat Tartlets.[10]

The seminar members also visited Turkey Hill Farm and Stewart's antique-filled, 1805 farmhouse. It was a setting easily recognized from many of the photographs in her books. The guests were seated in various dining areas throughout the first floor and served a festive lunch. Afterward, they were free to wander through the gardens, orchard, barn, and henhouse (with more than one hundred rare-breed chickens—some that lay pastel-colored eggs), and to enter a second barn (used for parties, not animals) for the next session, "Decorating Ideas."

During 1986, Stewart, along with Elizabeth Hawes, wrote the book *Weddings*, a guide for brides, mothers of brides, grooms, and anyone else interested in weddings. This gigantic book includes descriptions of actual weddings (many had been catered by Stewart), suggestions on how to prepare for this special event, and more than seven hundred photographs.

When *Weddings* was released in February 1987, with a first printing of seventy-five thousand copies, the tireless author set out on another cross-country book-signing tour. Again, reviewers made positive comments. A *Publishers Weekly* critic described the book as "bursting with intelligent nuptial advice and spectacular color photos."[11]

Unhappily, while Martha Stewart was off promoting *Weddings*, a disturbing change was about to take place in her own marriage. In the summer of 1987, Andy Stewart, whom she called "my best friend for twenty-seven years," moved out of their Turkey Hill home.[12] In speaking of their breakup, Martha said, "I noticed him growing away, but I didn't pay any attention to it. He said I was too much for him, that I was going too far too fast. . . . If I should be punished for being too critical or too perfectionist, I've been punished."[13] She has also said, "I'm sure he was tired of helping me. . . . I think he got tired of my drive."[14] A close friend of Andy

Stewart's said, "He told me he needed his own life . . . that he was building a business . . . and he needed the break to build his own life."[15] During their separation, Andy obtained a court order to keep them apart. They were not permitted to speak to each other or to enter each other's homes or offices.

Their separation and divorce, which became final in August 1990, was a difficult time for Martha Stewart. "It took five years and I think I'm pretty much over it," she told PBS talk-show host Charlie Rose, "The point is, I had work that kept me very interested."[16] In another interview, Stewart was asked if her marriage was a casualty of her phenomenal success. "I don't think it's the main reason we separated," she replied. "I think he changed, or wanted change, and I was happy with what I was doing."[17]

Despite the trauma in her personal life, Stewart was determined to carry on with her chosen work, saying, "What I write about is marriage and family, and I still believe in it all."[18]

In 1987, Kmart department stores signed Stewart to a $5 million, five-year contract as home-and-lifestyle consultant. She would introduce her own color line of Dutch Boy Paints and Martha Stewart linens and towels to Kmart shoppers. She would also produce a series of forty-three "At Home with Martha Stewart" commercials, to be aired on national television.

That same year, Stewart gave up the catering business to enable her to devote more time to her Kmart commitment and to write more books. *The Wedding Planner* was released early in 1988, followed by *Martha Stewart's Quick Cook Menus: Fifty-two Meals*

You Can Make in Under an Hour. One reviewer expressed doubt about the book's quick-cook claim. "Stewart's timetables really are impossible," she wrote, "unless you can debone two Cornish hens, rub them with spices and truss them, all in the five minutes she gives you for that task. While they bake you get to make Chinese dumplings from scratch. ('Trim with a fluted biscuit cutter, if desired.')"[19]

In the fall of 1988, Crown's president, Alan Mirken, asked Stewart if she would like to do a book on Christmas entertaining. She began to work on it right away, writing down family recipes and directions for making Christmas decorations and gifts. She invited photographer Christopher Baker to come to Turkey Hill right after Thanksgiving, to capture on film the family Christmas preparations, holiday party, and Christmas Day dinner. The result was *Martha Stewart's Christmas: Entertaining, Decorating, Giving*. Published in 1989, this colorful book is filled with ideas for the holiday season.

Martha Stewart's energy and enthusiasm drove her into more projects. In between book writing, she demonstrated some of her cooking and decorating methods on a series of four videotapes, *Martha Stewart's Secrets of Entertaining*, produced by Crown Video. Individual titles in the series are *A Formal Dinner Party, A Buffet Party for Family and Friends, An Antipasto Party*, and *A Holiday Feast for Thanksgiving and Other Festive Occasions*.

In 1989, Stewart's "Dinner Classics," a series of CDs and cassettes, were released. Martha Stewart selected the classical music to go with each of her

Martha Stewart shows how to prepare Thanksgiving dinner as part of her videotape series Martha Stewart's Secrets of Entertaining.

menus in the series. CBS Masterworks arranged the music, and a fold-in menu, complete with recipes, accompanied each album. By following the menu and recipes and playing the accompanying CD or cassette, a host or hostess could provide an entire evening of musical dining.

By 1990, Martha Stewart's eight books had sold more than two million copies.[20] "Everything I'm doing now I call the art of entertaining as it applies to the art of living," she said.[21]

6

Growth of
a Passion

For some time, in addition to writing books, Martha Stewart had been writing articles filled with more helpful information about enhancing everyday living. "The nineties are going to be more of a how-to decade than ever before," she said in a *House and Garden* magazine interview. "People are craving hard information."[1] How could she make this information available to a wider public?

At first, Stewart considered presenting the material in a series of how-to books, with contributions by other writers in addition to her own work. Unable to interest Crown, her book publisher, in this project, she turned to the idea of developing a magazine that would be filled with ideas for creating and maintaining a pleasant home lifestyle.[2]

Stewart approached several magazine publishers about her idea. Time Warner, Inc., made her an offer, which she accepted, to produce two test issues.[3] The first would go on sale November 12, 1990, and a second issue would follow on March 11, 1991. Then Time Warner would decide whether or not to launch *Martha Stewart Living* as either a monthly or a bimonthly (every two months).

The magazine was an immediate sellout, with 250,000 readers for the first issue. There was no doubt that *Martha Stewart Living* would continue to be published. In the magazine's third issue, July/August 1991, Martha Stewart thanked her readers for their "strong, positive response to the first two issues" and assured them that *Martha Stewart Living* would now be published regularly by Time Publishing Ventures, a division of Time Warner.[4] In the business agreement with Time, Stewart would receive an annual salary of $400,000, plus an expense account, and cash bonuses as the magazine's circulation and advertising accounts increased.[5]

Beginning in 1991, a segment of the magazine was aired on NBC-TV's *Today* show every other Wednesday morning. As host, Martha Stewart gave demonstrations on various topics ranging from bread baking and holiday treats to bulb planting and compost heaps. She appeared on the show without pay, in exchange for the publicity it brought to *Martha Stewart Living* magazine.[6]

Each issue of the magazine opens with "A Letter

from Martha," commenting on one or more of the topics presented in that issue. Also, readers are invited to suggest topics they would like to learn about.

The table of contents lists headings such as Good Things, Gardening, Cooking, Homekeeping, Restoring, Healing, and Financial Planning. Turning to the section on Good Things, one might find a professional chocolatier's step-by-step instructions for making perfect chocolates; under Restoring, an expert upholsterer shows how to reupholster furniture; under Healing, the reader learns about an herbal pharmacy.

Another feature is "Martha's Calendar." The entries on this full-page monthly calendar show Stewart's appointments, lecture dates, family and friends' birthdays, and around-the-home tasks, and may remind readers to do similar jobs around their own homes. A listing in January reads: Renew wardrobe; donate items no longer worn to charity. In April a date is scheduled to remove and clean storm windows; replace with screens. On October 29, two days before Halloween, Stewart plans to carve pumpkins and make candy apples.

Each issue ends with Stewart's "Remembering" column, sharing personal memories with her readers and, perhaps, stirring up memories of their own.

Despite heavy involvement as editor-in-chief of her own magazine and the need to prepare segments for the *Today* show, Stewart continued to write books. *Martha Stewart's Gardening, Month by Month* (1991) was her ninth book. In gathering material for it, she often worked at gardening twelve hours a day for weeks at a time. With such intense dedication,

Stewart has frequently been described as a workaholic and a perfectionist. "What motivates you to work so hard?" she was asked in a *Cosmopolitan* magazine interview. "I tend to get overenthusiastic, and often that's translated as workaholism," she replied. "I work at what I do, but to me it's fun. . . . Actually, I think I'd characterize myself more as an enthusiast than a perfectionist."[7]

Stewart's six-acre Turkey Hill Farm provided the setting for her gardening book. It described in detail an entire year of seasonal planting. For each of her planting projects, she kept a detailed account of the plant's progress. Its growth was clearly illustrated along with photos of Stewart, digging, hoeing, pruning, and transplanting. Included in the book were instructions on landscape design, soil improvement, and such garden-related projects as drying flowers, gilding pumpkins, and painting concrete planters.

Martha Stewart's Gardening, Month by Month was called "the ultimate garden journal" by one reviewer.[8] Its 360 pages included 650 color photographs by award-winning photographer Elizabeth Zeschin. In *The New York Times Book Review*, critic Allen Lacy described the book as "a helpful, sensible, authentic guide to the chores and the joys of a gardener's life, written by someone who doesn't mind if her hands get dirty," and then said, "Ms. Stewart writes with the authority that is won by long experience."[9] A reviewer for *Quill & Quire* was far more critical, calling the book a "flamboyant table-weight" and "a laughable failure as the gardening manual it purports to be."[10]

Seemingly tireless, Martha Stewart always had

several projects going on at the same time. This was the case with her restoration project. In 1988, she purchased a historic, run-down 152-year-old farmhouse in Westport as an investment. She planned to renovate, redesign, and redecorate the house, as well as landscape the grounds, thus creating a showcase of a nineteenth-century house designed for twentieth-century living.

George Christiansen, Martha's brother, was to be the contractor for this latest project. (George uses the last name of his wife, Rita.) For the next two years, Christiansen worked with a group of designers and skilled craftspeople, tearing apart, rebuilding, and redecorating the house.

All the while, Stewart and her mother kept detailed journals of this work-in-progress. Along the way, photographs were taken of the workers with close-ups of their implements and of the twenty-two rooms being decorated by twenty-seven designers. These journals and photographs were the basis for a series of articles that Stewart wrote for *Family Circle* magazine. The journals also provided material for her tenth book, *Martha Stewart's New Old House: Restoration, Renovation, Decoration,* which was published in 1992.

In the spring of 1990, after the farmhouse restoration was completed, Stewart joined with her neighbor, film star Paul Newman, to raise money for a special children's camp. She organized an event called "Homestyles: Trends and Traditions." During the month of May, her farmhouse was opened to the public. For an admission fee of $15, visitors could receive a guided tour of this unique, new-old house. All proceeds were donated to The Hole in the Wall Gang Camp in eastern Connecticut. Founded by Newman, it provides camp experiences for children with life-threatening diseases who might otherwise not have access to such activities.[11]

No matter what project captures Stewart's attention, it is usually recorded in writing. "I'm happiest working on books," she has said.[12] However, creating her art-book-quality cookbooks does not begin with writing. It begins with menus. First, Stewart decides on the menu for each meal that she plans to use. She must also decide on the setting in which the meal will be photographed—a dining room, a patio, a beach, or some other place. Next, the recipes are written and the food is prepared, arranged in a place setting, and photographed. Then the art director does a layout of the book. Layout refers to the way in which each page is arranged for ease of reading and for visual appeal. A decision is made where to place the recipe on a page, where the photographs are to be placed, and how much space will be available for the text. Finally, Stewart writes the text.

In her next book, *Martha Stewart's Menus for Entertaining* (1994), the text consists of a short essay by Stewart at the beginning of each of the twenty chapters. Each chapter includes a menu, the recipes needed for that menu, and a suggested table setting and flower arrangement. The book centers on themes suitable for entertaining, such as a North Carolina barbecue, a spicy Thai lunch, a Tuscan

"I'm happiest working on books," Martha Stewart has said. These are just a few of the lifestyle books and cookbooks she has written.

outdoor buffet, and, of course, ideas for celebrating special holidays.

Most of the menus were prepared and photographed at Stewart's Turkey Hill home or East Hampton summer place. Occasionally, the setting for a menu arose from a party given by friends. Such was the case with a crabs and corn on the beach menu. The event took place at the Long Island seaside home of friends and was photographed there.

Martha Stewart's gratitude for her friends'

generosity, and that of others, was expressed on the acknowledgments page of her book. This page at the opening of a book provides an opportunity for the author to express her thanks for the talent, hard work, and support of the associates and friends who participated in making the book become a reality.

Martha Stewart's Menus for Entertaining contains more than 150 recipes and was photographed in full color by Dana Gallagher. Stewart dedicated this book "To my mother, Martha Kostyra, on the occasion of her eightieth birthday."

Meanwhile, four years after its launching, *Martha Stewart Living* magazine was now a healthy success. With a circulation of twelve million copies per issue, Time Warner began to publish ten issues and two special issues annually.

The magazine staff began expanding into other areas as well. Its book publishing division gathered together "the best of" the holiday articles from the first three years of the magazine and published them in book form. The first "Best of *Martha Stewart Living*" book of these recycled articles was printed late in 1993 under the title *Holidays*. It includes recipes and ideas for gifts and decorations pertaining to Thanksgiving and Christmas. Martha Stewart's followers were instantly receptive. This nine-by-eleven-inch softcover book, with glossy pages and high-quality photos, sold more than 250,000 copies.[13]

Another "Best of *Martha Stewart Living*" book was published in 1994. Titled *Special Occasions*, it offers menus, recipes, and ideas for celebrating twelve special occasions. Some of these occasions are a New Year's

The "Best of Martha Stewart Living" *books are based on popular articles and ideas that have appeared in* Martha Stewart Living *magazine.*

Day soup buffet, a graduation day garden party in June, and an All Hallows' Eve potluck supper in October, along with instructions for carving pumpkins. This book, too, sold more than 250,000 copies.[14]

It had been five years since Martha Stewart conceived the idea of producing a magazine. Now, with two million readers, no one could have foreseen its tremendous growth. No one but its creator. "I wasn't surprised, because it was just right for the time," said Stewart in a speech at the National Press Club in Washington, D.C. "It worked because I started to bring back the idea of tradition, the idea of teaching, the idea of allowing us to feel good about decorating, about homekeeping, about collecting, about restoring."[15]

There are other theories about the reason for the popularity of Stewart's homekeeping and gardening ideas. Some people attribute it to the "cocooning" trend—the tendency of people to spend more time at home because of economic reasons. Unable to afford the luxury of travel, entertainment, or elaborate dinners out, their attention is focused more on the home.

A New York–based trend spotter, Faith Popcorn, has suggested that many people today "are enjoying homemaking more as a voyeuristic experience. . . . They like knowing how to do something without actually having to do it. Learning to wire a lamp is fascinating. But you don't have to actually rewire one."[16]

According to Bernard Beck, associate professor of sociology at Northwestern University, "There's been a major change in the economic organization in the work world. . . . People are retiring early and they need a whole new approach to life. They're becoming interested in domesticity again."[17]

Whatever the trend or the reason, Martha Stewart has clearly tapped into it and added to its growth. With the resounding success of her books and the *Martha Stewart Living* magazine, the master of style was now ready to carry her ideas of tradition and homekeeping even further.

New
Ventures

Until 1993, much of Martha Stewart's communication with the public had been through books, lectures, and magazines. Her biweekly appearances on NBC-TV's *Today*, however, and in Kmart commercials, had given her nationwide visibility and brought ever-growing attention to her magazine and books.

The *Martha Stewart Living* staff now began to move into the area of television production as a secondary venture. They started in a modest way by producing a series of thirty-minute programs to air once a week, with Stewart as host.

Stewart's series would include cooking instructions as well as other home-related information. Its purpose was to inspire viewers to try the recipes and projects suggested. "I love showing people how to do things," Stewart told CNN's Larry King, during a home decorating session. She believes, "The more that people know how these things were done, the more they'll be able to apply it to their own lives."[1]

In September 1993, *Martha Stewart Living*, a weekly syndicated television program, made its debut. It appeared at 8:30 on Sunday mornings throughout the country. The *Martha Stewart Living* program demonstrates many interesting projects that can be done around the house—gardening, cooking, decorating, entertaining. The program soon gathered an enthusiastic audience, not only of women but of men and children as well.

The show opens to the sound of lively music and fleeting shots of Martha Stewart planting a rose bush, gathering multicolored zinnias into a wicker basket, fishing aboard a boat in the Long Island Sound, or engaged in some other spirited activity. "Good Morning. Welcome," might be her greeting that day. "I'm so glad you could join us." The viewer is then told what to expect on that day's program. A typical show features about four topics, under such general headings as Cooking, Gardening, Crafts, Good Things, Projects, Field Trips—topics similar to those covered in the magazine.

One of the attractions of the show is that it is not taped in a TV studio. Much of the videotaping takes place at Stewart's Turkey Hill compound in Westport. Here, in her country kitchen, amid copper pots and hanging baskets, the bulk of the cooking is done on an oversized stove. The viewer doesn't have to imagine the garden or the fruit trees from which the vegetables and fruit are harvested. The audience is there in the orchard with Stewart, as she stands on a ladder picking "dead ripe" sour cherries from the Montmorency cherry tree for the homemade cherry preserves that she will soon prepare. Next, the viewer is in the kitchen with Stewart and Salli LaGrone, a cook from Nashville, Tennessee, who has come to visit and will help in today's project. Both are wearing chef's aprons, and Salli pits cherries in an ingenious cherry pitter that Stewart recently discovered. With a calm voice and unhurried manner, Stewart explains each step of the recipe—mixing cherries, sugar, and fresh lemon juice in a huge cooking pot, boiling, adding pectin, and boiling a minute more. Salli helps with ladling the preserves into sterilized canning jars and sealing them.

The you-are-there quality of the show transports the viewer from his or her own sometimes-stressful world to one more tranquil and orderly. Hens cluck and roosters crow as Stewart enters the chicken house to gather fresh eggs from her more than one hundred hens of many varieties. (The imported Araucana variety produce pastel blue and green eggs.) A fluffy, cream-colored cat strolls through the garden as her mistress, in purple T-shirt and jeans, kneels beside a newly dug trench, ready to demonstrate the proper way to plant asparagus.

At other times the viewer is taken on field trips to such places as a green market in New York City, where fresh-grown fruit and vegetables are brought in daily by nearby growers; to an antique shop in Connecticut, to browse among eighteenth- and nineteenth-century artifacts; or, in December, to hunt for a Christmas tree at a tree farm managed by the Audubon Society.

Infomercials appear between segments of the program. These differ from the regular commercials, which are paid for by outside advertisers. The infomercials are advertisements directly related to the *Martha Stewart Living* program. For example, in an ad promoting the *Martha Stewart Living* magazine, Stewart tells of a special offer. New subscribers will receive three gift booklets: "Good Things" from the kitchen, from the garden, and for the holidays. "It's a ri-*dic*-ulously good thing," says Martha Stewart.

Other infomercials offer assorted Martha By Mail products, such as a cake decorating kit, or large handcrafted, copper cookie cutters. These are shown packaged with Martha Stewart's logo—a beehive—on each box. At the end of each infomercial, a toll-free telephone number is given for placing orders.

In addition to hosting her own weekly television show, Stewart continued to make biweekly appearances on NBC-TV's *Today*. In December 1994, she visited the White House and interviewed First Lady Hillary Rodham Clinton. Soon after, an account of her visit was shared with co-anchors Katie Couric and Bryant Gumbel and their *Today* show audience.

In her interview, Stewart asked the First Lady how involved she had been in holiday preparations at the White House. Mrs. Clinton explained that they start planning for the next Christmas a year in advance, first deciding on a theme. That year's theme was the carol "Twelve Days of Christmas," which is one of the First Family's favorites.[2] After a tour of the White House, Stewart remarked, "I think you've done a really wonderful job in maintaining a family atmosphere here. Do you feel like it's your home?"

"Well, we do," the First Lady replied, "and that was very important to me. One of the primary goals I had was to make sure that my husband and my daughter felt at home. Although this is the people's house and it's a museum, and it's a great place where wonderful matters of state occur, it is our home."[3]

Another venture for Stewart and her staff was her first prime-time television special. Titled *Martha Stewart's Home for the Holidays*, it aired on Tuesday night, December 12, 1995, on CBS-TV. The one-hour show featured First Lady Hillary Clinton, with whom Stewart hung a Christmas wreath. Culinary expert Julia Child was featured in a dessert-making session, and Miss Piggy of the Muppets joined hostess Stewart in building a gingerbread house.

The following year Martha Stewart produced her second prime-time television Christmas special, *Welcome Home for the Holidays*. The one-hour program aired on December 10, 1996. One of the guests, basketball superstar Michael Jordan, was shown visiting a New York Athletic Club children's party, where he placed a star on top of the Christmas tree. Actor Dennis Franz, of television's *NYPD Blue*, dropped by Stewart's Turkey Hill home, along with his wife, for a cup of holiday punch. Miss Piggy, as a returning guest from Stewart's 1995 Christmas special, offered

Miss Piggy helps Martha Stewart get ready for the holidays on her prime-time CBS-TV special Welcome Home for the Holidays.

her own unique comments while her hostess decorated cookies to hang on the tree.

How do Martha Stewart and the *Martha Stewart Living* staff prepare for the holidays? Like First Lady Hillary Clinton, they begin to think about the next Christmas right after the current one. With a staff of about ninety, including full-time editors, stylists, photographers, and writers, the ideas come from everyone. "We're all working together," Stewart has said. "We have our little Santa's workshop going twenty-four hours a day, twelve months a year. So, we have a lot of sessions where we come up with ideas."[4]

Actually, they have several Christmases to consider. To avoid duplication, they need different holiday features for each venture—the magazine, books, and television special. The shooting has to be done months earlier, when the temperature is far different from the scenes they need to photograph. For the 1996 Christmas special—filmed in September and October—the crew had to install fake snow. The twenty-nine Christmas trees that were needed for winter scenery had to be cut early in the fall at a tree farm.[5]

Meanwhile, the *Martha Stewart Living* syndicated television show continued to grow in popularity. In June 1995, the thirty-minute show began appearing in reruns five mornings a week on cable-TV's Lifetime channel. Reaching more than five million viewers across the country each week, it made Martha Stewart's name even more familiar.

Letters of praise arrived daily at the *Martha Stewart Living* office in New York. "Thanks for giving me something to look forward to on television," wrote

Television star Dennis Franz, of NYPD Blue, *joins Martha Stewart in 1996 for a cup of holiday cheer on* Welcome Home for the Holidays.

a New Jersey viewer.[6] "I even had cable installed so I could watch your show on Lifetime," wrote another, from Mobile, Alabama.[7] An eleven-year-old from British Columbia wrote, "I hardly ever watch TV, but if I do, your show is one I try not to miss."[8]

Stewart had begun doing business with Time Warner in 1990 with the launching of *Martha Stewart Living* magazine. By 1993, she had three million books in print, a weekly television show in 84 percent of the nation's viewing markets, and a magazine selling half a million copies an issue.[9] She had come a long way, but wanted to go further. It was time to think about a new deal in which she would have more control over her products.

In all of her previous professional transactions, Stewart had never had an official business manager. Prior to her divorce, Andy Stewart had provided some legal advice in negotiating book contracts. Afterward, she had no professional business advisors to guide her in making decisions. Stewart now assembled a trio of high-powered financial consultants—Charlotte Beers, Sharon Patrick, and entertainment lawyer Allen Grubman. Under their guidance throughout a year of negotiation, Stewart and Time Warner reached an agreement.

In 1995, Time Warner created a new corporation called Martha Stewart Living Enterprises. Martha Stewart was named chairman and chief executive officer (CEO). The new company would be a partnership, jointly owned by Time Inc. Ventures and by Martha Stewart. She was now in charge of both the business and the creative side of her many activities within Time Warner. This arrangement gave Stewart more control, but she still was not the sole owner of her business activities.

Martha Stewart Living Enterprises included a publishing division (the magazine and related books), a television division (syndicated television programs), and *Today* show segments. It also included an interactive-media division (to investigate future participation in Internet, CD-ROM, and telemarketing), and a merchandising division (to plan a possible Martha Stewart catalog or a chain of Martha Stewart stores).[10]

Not included in the Martha Stewart Living Enterprises agreement were her lectures and her non-magazine-related books. Starting with *Entertaining* in 1982, Clarkson N. Potter had published all of Stewart's books. In 1995, they published another cookbook.

Encouraged by her publisher and assisted by the publisher's staff, Stewart compiled all of her recipes and cooking and baking techniques into one volume. More than sixteen hundred recipes appear in *The Martha Stewart Cookbook: Collected Recipes for Every Day*. Unlike her previous art-quality books, this one is an all-purpose cookbook. Although lacking the usual color photographs of her previous books, it is filled with culinary information. A reviewer for *Library Journal* suggested that Stewart's fans would welcome the book "as a resource and a reference."[11]

This was Martha Stewart's thirteenth book. On the acknowledgments page she wrote, "I am thrilled that I have had the pleasure of collaborating with so many talented, creative, and hard-working people."

8

On the Go

Beginning with the publication of Stewart's first book, *Entertaining*, she had gone on a nationwide book-signing tour to promote each new book. The early tours were modestly attended because she was relatively unknown west of the Hudson River. In 1993, after she began appearing each week on her own television show, the demand for her books vastly increased. At a *Menus for Entertaining* book signing in San Francisco in 1994, almost a thousand readers lined up for Stewart's autograph.

As the demand for her books increased, so did the requests for personal appearances and lectures. At first, she gave several lectures a week, but she had to cut back to about one a month because of an increase in her other business activities.

Stewart's lectures are presented to groups whose proceeds go to benefit their local charities. "I am thrilled," she said, "to participate in fund-raisers that actually put real money to excellent use in the community."[1] In giving her talks, Stewart uses slides, many of which show photographs from her books and magazine, and chooses those that apply to the particular interest of the group that she is addressing. "If it's a community where gardens are prevalent, I'll talk about gardening, and my gardening books will be featured," she explained. "If it's a lecture on restoration, we'll feature my *New Old House*."[2]

Stewart has about a dozen lectures prepared and revises them to fit the occasion. The event usually involves a special breakfast for the patrons—the major contributors to that particular fund-raising charity. This is followed by Stewart's lecture, and a luncheon, for which those in attendance have paid somewhere between $35 and $75. The food for these occasions is prepared and served by a local caterer. Afterward, a traditional book signing takes place for those who would like an autographed copy of one of Stewart's books.

Long before the event, the organizers have arranged for a local bookseller to display and sell a selection of Martha Stewart's books on the day of her lecture. A portion of the profit from book sales goes to the charity. As many as eight hundred to nine hundred books are often sold at these affairs.[3]

Stewart gives ten to fifteen charity lectures each

year, for which she receives $15,000 apiece. There is usually a waiting list. Members of a Junior League in Washington State applied almost two years in advance for Stewart to speak at their 1997 fund-raiser. Apparently, it was worth the wait. Dedicated fans arrived from as far away as California and Alaska. Waiting in the book-signing line after the ninety-minute lecture, a young woman from Seattle said, "My whole life consists of Martha tips. I made a turkey from her Turkey 101 instructions in her magazine and got rave reviews."[4]

At Marshall Field's department store in Chicago, three hundred fans lined up to hear Martha Stewart's bridal talk and to buy a signed copy of her book. One woman, who had skipped work and waited in line more than two hours, spoke glowingly of her idol. "Martha is a woman of the nineties," she said. "She's made an empire. She's a role model."[5]

Not everyone loves Martha Stewart. A *New York Times* article labeled her "Public Enemy No. 1."[6] The *Boston Globe* featured her as "The Hostess from Hell,"[7] and *Lear's* magazine asked, "Is Martha Stewart Good for America?"[8] It is said that she is tough to work with—that she is bossy.

Despite the criticism, there are plenty of admirers who are ready to listen and learn and add something new to their lives. While acknowledging that Stewart is indeed "bossy," the editor of *House & Garden* countered that "she knows what's good for us."[9] Stewart is often requested to give handcraft demonstrations at her lectures and other guest appearances. On the *Larry King Live* show on CNN, she created a Thanksgiving

As the demand for Martha Stewart's books increased, so did the requests for personal appearances. Here she attends the reopening of Warner Bros. Studio Store, accompanied by Bugs Bunny.

centerpiece from a copper-gilded pumpkin and an assortment of dried plants and berries. On a morning segment of *Live With Regis and Kathie Lee*, she demonstrated the making of Christmas table favors. On MSNBC, she showed how to assemble a gift kit for growing narcissus.

At a Kmart opening on Long Island, Stewart gave demonstrations on wreath decorating and the marbleizing of Christmas ornaments. In Las Vegas, at a fund-raiser for cancer research, she conducted a wreath workshop in which both women and men participated. "Lots of people were there making wreaths, sitting there enjoying themselves," said Stewart. "And we sent them home with the wreath kits and everything. . . . It was an awful lot of fun."[10]

Wreath making was an especially familiar activity for Stewart in 1996. After her visit to the White House the previous year, and seeing holiday decorations sent by individuals from all over America, she came up with a wreath idea. Why not create a wreath to represent each of our nation's fifty states?[11]

The Martha Stewart Living staff began to research the kind of material and design that would be appropriate for each state. They also included the District of Columbia and the United States territories (the islands of Guam and American Samoa in the Pacific and Puerto Rico in the Caribbean).

After a year of intense, creative work, fifty-two wreaths were presented in a "Best of *Martha Stewart Living*" book called *Great American Wreaths*, published in 1996. Each wreath is made up of material native to the particular state or territory it represents.

To use material that was as authentic as possible, the *Martha Stewart Living* staff had gathered information from forest rangers, agriculture departments, nursery growers, and farmers in the various states. The result was fifty-two unique wreaths displaying the distinctive natural products of each state.

For Vermont, sugar-maple leaves were used; for Oklahoma, winter wheat; sagebrush for New Mexico; apples and pears for Oregon; and so on. Not all the wreaths were designed in a traditional circle. Some were fashioned into a garland (a long strip of foliage) or into a swag (a garland fastened at each end and hanging down in the middle).

For Louisiana, magnolia leaves were woven into one long garland, to be draped over an entrance. For Ohio, seventy-five buckeye nuts were threaded with brass wire, gathered in a cluster, like a bunch of grapes, and hung from a wide, gold ribbon. An enormous square wreath of citrus fruits represented the state of Florida.

An oak-leaf and gilded-acorn wreath of impressive size was designed for the District of Columbia. After Martha Stewart presented the wreath to First Lady Hillary Clinton, they hung it on the iron balustrade (decorative railing) of the South Portico of the White House.[12]

The *Great American Wreaths* book is filled with lavish color photographs. Step-by-step instructions make it possible for the reader to duplicate each design. An added feature is the background information included about the seeds, grass, berries, leaves, and other natural products of each state. A two-page map of the

United States and its territories, and a glossary of the products of each area, add to the book's appeal as a reference source.

Publication of the "Best of *Martha Stewart Living*" books, with articles and ideas that have appeared in past issues of the magazine, continues. *Handmade Christmas* was published in 1995, with ideas for creating gifts, candles, ornaments, and other holiday items—even for designing gift wrapping paper.

Two more "best of" books were published in 1996. *What to Have for Dinner* presents thirty-two easy menus for every night of the week. *How to Decorate* is a guide to creating comfortable, stylish living spaces. Some of the changes made in Stewart's own homes are shown. The work of her daughter, Alexis Stewart, is also displayed, including an apartment she designed for Susan Magrino, Martha Stewart's publicist and longtime friend.

In 1997, the book *Good Things*, a collection of household ideas and projects, was published. It provides instructions for more than two hundred "good things" that readers can create for themselves or as gifts.

That same year Stewart brought out another book, *Martha Stewart's Healthy Quick Cook*. In this collection of fifty-two easy menus, the recipes are fashioned for the more health-conscious, low-fat dining of today. Beautiful color photographs accompany each menu. This was the first of Stewart's books to be published under the direction of her new company, Martha Stewart Living Omnimedia.

Living—Her Way

Martha Stewart has been described as being so driven that work is her whole life.[1] Does she ever have time for other parts of her life?

"My life is my work, and my work is my life," she explained at a National Press Club luncheon in Washington, D.C., in November 1996. "And, that it involves the home, the family, the gardens, everything else involved in living, is my luck. . . . I can think about my work twenty-four hours a day and it's pleasant."[2]

As a corporate executive, Stewart has much to accomplish every day. Rising about 5:00 A.M., she walks the dogs, feeds the chickens (baby cracked

Martha Stewart was a featured guest speaker at the National Press Club luncheon in Washington, D.C., in November 1996.

corn, mash, and greenery from the garden), feeds the cats, changes the kitty litter, and often phones her friends at this early hour. At 6:00 A.M., a professional trainer arrives to supervise her workout of stretching, weight lifting, and aerobics. Whenever time allows, she also keeps fit by bicycling, fast walking, and in-line skating.

After breakfast, Stewart makes lists of what needs to be done and confers with her staff before taking off for the day's appointments. In her home office, a computer, printer, modem, fax machine, and phone keep her in touch with the *Martha Stewart Living* headquarters in New York City. Much of the time she travels to her appointments in a black Mercedes, driven by longtime driver and assistant Larry Kennedy. As he drives, she works in the backseat, which is equipped with a portable phone, laptop computer, and other office necessities.

She frequently travels out of town for lectures and book signings but tries to spend most nights at home. Stewart has much writing and reading to do. She reads numerous books on how to do things, consults with experts, and conducts experiments at home on new methods and ideas. She admits to needing hardly more than four hours of sleep and sometimes reads through the night.

Stewart's family has no problem understanding her nonstop drive. They are convinced that her ambition comes from her perfectionist father, who died in 1979. In gardening, Edward Kostyra competed with a neighbor in trying to grow the longest beans, recalls his widow, Martha Kostyra. He corrected the spelling in letters and returned them to the senders. He was "supercritical," says Stewart's older brother Eric. "It's a family curse."[3] Martha Stewart agrees. "My father was a real perfectionist. . . . I think I get that from him. And I think I get the stick-to-itiveness from my mother."[4]

When she is not traveling to a lecture or a book signing, Stewart divides her time between her Turkey Hill home in Westport and her summer house on Lily Pond Lane in East Hampton, New York. The rambling, cedar-shingled beach house, close to the shore of Long Island Sound, has twelve bedrooms, long, shady porches, and a trellised rose garden. Like her Westport home, this house often provides the setting for the photographs in her books, magazine, and television shows. The roomy kitchen is equipped with several stoves, deep marble sinks, wide marble counters, and many storage cupboards. Stewart also has an apartment on Fifth Avenue in Manhattan, a convenient stopover between city business meetings.

Martha Stewart's family is very much a part of her work as well as her personal life. Various members have appeared in segments of her television show, in videos, books, and the magazine. Stewart's brother George can be seen carving the Thanksgiving turkey in her holiday entertaining video. Nieces and nephews have assisted with the decorating and tree trimming in each of her televised Christmas specials. Individual family members are frequently mentioned in her "Remembering" column of the magazine. Her sister-in-law Rita Christiansen, wife of brother George, is business manager of her Westport office.

In one of Stewart's televised shows, her sister Laura Plimpton did a segment on collecting Depression glass (glass tableware produced in the United States between 1920 and 1940). In another, their mother (known in the family as Big Martha), demonstrated her own method of making stollen, a sweetened German bread containing raisins, nuts, and citron. Big Martha, who was eighty at the time, is much shorter than her five-foot-nine-inch daughter. Despite her small size, though, one observer noted that in the process of pounding and rolling the stollen, Big Martha seemed to have the power of ten men. "You see where I get my strength from," Martha Stewart has said.[5]

Stewart's pets are also involved in her work life, and her five cats and three chow dogs are often mentioned in the magazine. When *Martha Stewart Living* magazine began a family pet column titled "Caring," one of Stewart's chows, Pawpaw, and three of her Himalayan cats, Beethoven, Teeny, and Weeny, were whisked to appointments at Linda's Doggie Salon in nearby Stratford, Connecticut. They were to serve as models for a pet-grooming article to be published in the magazine.[6]

Daughter Alexis plays a large part in her mother's life and enjoys many of the same interests. A Barnard College graduate and a businesswoman, she is interested in home design and is a contributor to the magazine. Her renovation of an 1870s East Hampton carriage house into a summer cottage was included in *How to Decorate*, one of the "Best of *Martha Stewart Living*" books (1996).[7]

Martha Stewart with Pawpaw, one of her three chow dogs. Stewart's pets often model for her magazine.

Alexis Stewart owns and has successfully remodeled the Bridgehampton Motel, not far from her mother's Long Island summer house. She also owns a shop in East Hampton called Yard Sale. She and her mother go to movies, eat Japanese food, and browse antique shops and bookstores together. "They're truly close," says a family friend, "and Alexis hates it when people criticize Martha."[8]

In November 1997, Alexis married attorney John Cuti. It was a small private wedding. According to a friend, Martha would have loved to have a big event, but this is what Alexis wanted, so Martha was happy.[9] Her gift to the newlyweds was a New York City apartment, and she dedicated her book *Martha Stewart's Healthy Quick Cook* "To Alexis Stewart and John Cuti: 'Recipes to Share.'"

As with many celebrities, Martha Stewart is often the focus of unflattering stories, many of which are either made up or exaggerated. Stewart's fans know that she is enthusiastic and caring about raising chickens. She is often seen feeding them or collecting their eggs from inside her Westport henhouse. Stewart did not seem amused by a parody published in *Spy* magazine. (A parody is a humorous imitation of something, often intended to ridicule that person.) According to the story, Martha Stewart had placed a bag of baby chicks in her driveway and had run over the bag with her Mercedes. "That's ridiculous and totally untrue," she told a feature writer for *New York* magazine. "Most people would love to come back as my chicken."[10]

Several parodies have been written about Stewart,

two of them in book form. In one, a Martha Stewart look-alike is pictured sedately walking on water while serving her garden party guests. At times, Stewart finds such humor amusing, as with a cartoon by Roz Chast in *The New Yorker* magazine. Captioned "Martha Stewart Takes Over the Universe," it showed her handing out party ideas on the planets Pluto and Mars. "That woman should be given an award," said Stewart.[11]

When these stories become mean-spirited, she admits they are troubling. "I'm trying to share my knowledge, my interest . . . It makes me a little bit sad that they're not quite getting it."[12]

Julia Child seems to agree. After having had Stewart as her guest on a PBS-TV segment of *Baking at Julia's*, Child said, "We were all delighted with her. I don't know why people are so mean about her. Probably because she's so successful."[13]

When questioned about a recent unflattering, unauthorized biography of herself and about other critical press, Stewart said, "I think people are sort of astonished that a homemaker can go out and build an over-a-million-dollar-company. But this is not so unusual in America. So instead of talking about how great it is that a woman has gone out and from scratch done something amazing . . . I'm vilified."[14]

Fans of Stewart, however, seem unaffected by any of these attacks on their lifestyle expert. Groups of women throughout the country have organized Martha Stewart clubs—gathering to watch her television shows, to work on one of her projects, or to prepare a luncheon or dinner menu from one of her shows or her books.

In 1994, Stewart appeared as a guest on the syndicated TV show *Oprah*, along with a group of "Martha Stewart's Wannabees and Wannanots." The "Wannabees," including Alice Probst, president of a 250-member Martha Stewart Fan Club, praised Stewart and told of the various ways in which she had influenced their lives. "The thing I like about Martha," said Ms. Probst, "is she appreciates her family and her friends. And she does what she can to . . . make them feel like maybe you did something a little extra, a little special." [15]

In contrast, the "Wannanots" told of feeling pressured in not being able to measure up to Stewart's standards. How could she do it all on her own?

Realistically, Martha Stewart can not and does not run a corporation and several residences on her own. For many years, she resisted hiring household help. "We never had any help at home, so it never occurred to me that I shouldn't do it all," she once said about her early years as a wife, mother, and caterer. [16] Now, however, she must concentrate on running a major business that requires her to be gone from home for long periods of time. To keep her house running smoothly and the garden tended, she has several employees, including two housekeepers, two gardeners, two kitchen assistants, and in her Westport office, a four-person staff.

Occasionally, Stewart takes a vacation break, usually the week after Christmas, and she chooses faraway, adventurous destinations: trekking up

Mount Kilimanjaro, a volcanic peak in northeast Tanzania, or sportfishing for tarpon, a large game fish, off the coast of Costa Rica. On a chartered boat tour of the Galapagos Islands off the coast of Ecuador, Stewart was accompanied by four nieces and nephews, two godchildren, and two adult friends.

The Martha Stewart seen on television has a trim, casual look. She usually wears no-nonsense, working-at-home clothes—jeans or slacks topped with a tailored shirt, its rolled-up sleeves revealing a large, practical watch on her left arm. Her short, blond hair looks slightly tousled. Her brown eyes have a direct gaze, and diamond studs glisten from her pierced ears. Although Stewart is known to wear designer clothes in her business life, her personal approach to clothes seems to be casual. "I like to shop for food," she once told Oprah Winfrey, "but not for clothes."[17]

Does Martha Stewart have a social life? She dates often, and her friends say she is a wonderful companion.[18] Would she ever marry again? "Sure, I want to be married again," she said in a television interview with PBS talk-show host Charlie Rose. "I don't want to have a life alone with a good movie."[19]

Meanwhile, in Martha Stewart's fast-paced, daily life, what doesn't she have that she wants? "It is T-I-M-E," she responds at once. "I do so many things. The day is too short. I find, no matter how early I get up or how late I go to bed, there's not enough time to do everything I really want to do."[20]

Riding
on Success

With the creation of Martha Stewart Living Enterprises in 1995, headed by Martha Stewart as chairman and CEO, her rise to power had become a twentieth-century American success story. From her modest beginning as a caterer working from her home, then writing the book *Entertaining* based on that experience, she dedicated herself to enhancing the home lifestyle of others. In sharing ideas and information with readers and viewers, she had built a multimillion-dollar business.

In June 1996, *Time* magazine listed Martha Stewart as one of "America's 25 Most Influential People." Calling her an "empress of 'How-To,'" *Time* referred to Stewart as "simply Martha: cooking, sewing, gilding, planting, wallpapering, and painting her way into every corner of your house—and your life."[1]

Six months later, on an ABC-TV television special, Barbara Walters introduced Martha Stewart as "The Most Fascinating Business Person of the Year." Following a clip showing the two women decorating cookies, Walters asked, "Don't you give someone like me an inferiority complex?" "I don't want you to have an inferiority complex," said Stewart. "I just want you to fill your mind, whenever you have a free moment, with great ideas, with great information, with a *little* bit of inspiration."[2] Filling her own mind with great ideas, information, and inspiration, along with hard work, could have been the formula that drove Stewart to become a successful businesswoman, but had she reached her goal?

At that time, Stewart was rumored to be in the process of buying Martha Stewart Living Enterprises from Time Warner. She wanted to be the owner of her own business. Back in 1995, when Martha Stewart Living Enterprises was created, Time Warner continued to provide the financing, so it still owned the company. Now, with the extraordinary growth of the magazine and the ever-growing popularity of the *Martha Stewart Living* television show, Stewart began to push for more control over the company that she had helped create. As chairman and CEO of Martha Stewart Living Enterprises, she had proved to herself that she could run a company. She believed the time had come for her to own it. "I should own my name. I should own my copyright. I should own my business."[3]

Martha Stewart's rise to power is a twentieth-century American success story.

In the spring of 1996, many business discussions took place between the executives of Time Warner and Stewart's own financial advisors. Although there was much speculation on Wall Street about what might be taking place, both sides declined to comment. A *Wall Street Journal* article suggested that Stewart had become "a world-class headache for Time" and wrote of her "alleged tendency to act like a prima donna and live like a mogul."[4]

Immediately, letters to the editor appeared in her defense. Wrote one reader, "I don't see why the lady needs to be labeled a 'world-class headache' for Time Warner just because she's waking up to the fact that to control her own destiny she needs to 'get a nice big piece of the action for herself.' " Another wrote, "Time Warner seems reluctantly aware that without Martha Stewart, the magazine and related ventures would be of little value."[5]

On February 4, 1997, after nearly a year of negotiation, Stewart announced the formation of a new company, Martha Stewart Living Omnimedia. She had been able to raise enough money to buy out most of Time, Inc.'s stake in the company.[6]

Stewart's purchase included the *Martha Stewart Living* magazine; her syndicated television show; books written by her and the editors of *Martha Stewart Living*; a syndicated weekly newspaper column, "Ask Martha"; and a mail-order catalog company, Martha By Mail.[7] Under the agreement, Time Warner would retain an interest of less than 20 percent in all the Martha Stewart ventures but would continue to work with her in distributing *Martha Stewart Living* magazine.

As chairman and chief executive officer of Martha Stewart Living Omnimedia, Stewart named management consultant Sharon Patrick as chief operating officer of the company. Known for her negotiating skill, Patrick was a major figure in completing the transaction for the new company. With a staff of competent associates, Stewart undertook to develop, among other innovations, a Martha Stewart on-line service and to create radio programming that would offer useful "how to" information in ninety-second segments.

September 8, 1997, was the first day of the new daily television program, *Martha Stewart Living Weekdays* and *Martha Stewart Living Weekend*. These thirty-minute programs feature all new projects, cooking demonstrations, and field trips.

Also on September 8, the Martha Stewart Web site <www.marthastewart.com> made its debut. The site provides a program guide for the television show, tips and recipes from the show, and a preview clip of the next episode. By entering the site and registering, the visitor also gains access to E-mail, transcripts from "Ask Martha" (the ninety-second radio spots), and other offerings as they are added. The Web site has not been praised as widely as some of Stewart's other endeavors. A *Wall Street Journal* reporter called it "more disorganized than a closetful of crumpled-up table linens," but did note that Stewart had stated her plans to improve the site.[8]

First and foremost, Stewart considered Martha Stewart Living Omnimedia to be an educational company. "We are 'Omnimedia.' . . . stretching across all fields of the media. . . . I think that we really want to teach and I think that we're doing a good job at it already. The magazine certainly teaches a tremendous amount of information to people."[9]

In informing *Martha Stewart Living* magazine's readers about the plans of Martha Stewart Living Omnimedia, Stewart said, "Our goal is to teach, to inform, and to inspire all of you in the preservation and extension of traditional family values and activities."[10]

Another change taking place in 1997 was Stewart's move from her popular, twice-monthly television appearances on NBC-TV's *Today* show, to a once-a-week spot on CBS-TV's *This Morning*. According to Stewart, the reason for the switch was that CBS offered both more money and more airtime than NBC did.[11] The switch took place on February 11, 1997, with Stewart featured every Tuesday morning in a segment on cooking, gardening, or other homekeeping project.

About the same time, Stewart announced a new three-year agreement with Kmart, launching a brand-new bed, bath, and paint line. Under the label "Martha Stewart Everyday," she would design sheets and towels for Kmart's bed and bath department. Also, under the brand name "Martha Stewart Everyday Colors," she would develop, through the Sherwin-Williams Corporation, a line of interior and exterior house paint that would be available to Kmart shoppers. Some of the paint colors were inspired by the pastel eggshells produced by her Araucana chickens.

As a result of the increase in television programming,

Martha Stewart and other celebrities attended a 1997 meeting in Albany, New York, to promote state funding for the arts. Here she speaks with Earle I. Mack, chairman of the New York State Council on the Arts.

more daily shows would need to be filmed and an area more spacious than the Turkey Hill house would be needed. Television production requires many workers at the site of the filming, as well as bulky trucks and vans transporting camera equipment. Some Westport residents had complained about film crews blocking traffic around Turkey Hill Road.

In December 1997, construction was completed on Stewart's new television studio complex. Included are enlarged versions of both her East Hampton kitchen (studio A), and her Westport kitchen (studio B). There is also a dining area for catered staff lunches and a fully equipped gym. Much of the filming for Stewart's television shows as well as the taping for her radio shows, is now done in these studios. Turkey Hill farm, however, remains the setting for her gardening segments.

Except for the field trips shown on *Martha Stewart Living*, segments of the thirty-minute programs are often filmed on the premises of Stewart's homes. Some form of work—cooking, sewing, flower arranging, wreath making, or "Good Things" projects—takes place for television demonstration in various rooms of these homes almost every day. Stewart has stenciled floors, painted rooms, restored old kitchen chairs, and built window boxes.

For Stewart, her homes are her laboratories— places to experiment with food and paints and projects, and places from which to teach her viewers and readers. Even her New York City apartment provided a showcase of what can be done to make the most of limited kitchen space. In a remodeling project planned by Stewart, her efficient "galley alley" was photographed and described in *How to Decorate*, a "Best of *Martha Stewart Living*" book (1996).[12]

In 1991, Stewart bought a thirty-five-acre estate in Fairfield, Connecticut, a town next to Westport. The 1920s colonial-style house is surrounded by woodlands and rolling fields. A pond and stream add country charm to the natural setting. Stewart plans to do a series of books based on the development of this vast acreage.

Reaching out for another new project from which to learn and develop new ideas, Stewart purchased a house in East Hampton in 1995. Designed by the late architect Gordon Bunshaft, the flat-roofed, rectangular structure is located on more than an acre of land overlooking Georgica Pond. Its modern, concrete exterior is in sharp contrast to the hearth-and-home image of Martha Stewart. However, true to her nature, she has remodeling plans for this three-room house with its windowless, undersized kitchen. Working with architect Walter Chatham, who had designed her Manhattan apartment, she plans to turn one of the rooms into "a nice big open kitchen . . . full of light and air. I'll be able to cook there to my heart's content."[13]

In September 1997, Stewart purchased a sixty-one-acre estate in Seal Harbor, Maine, located on Mount Desert Island. After Long Island and Martha's Vineyard, Mount Desert is the third largest island on the East Coast. Known as Skylands, the three-story stone mansion on Stewart's property includes twelve bedrooms.[14]

Like her Turkey Hill and East Hampton homes,

perhaps these new houses, too, will eventually be seen in *Martha Stewart Living* magazine, in one of Stewart's books, or on *Martha Stewart Living* television.

Even in her fifties, Stewart retains her fashion-model good looks. In May 1996, she was selected by *People* magazine as one of "The 50 Most Beautiful People in the World." Her attractiveness, however, did not create her business success. Says one of her friends, Mort Zuckerman, chairman of *U.S. News & World Report*, "Martha is a unique combination of the beauty of the orchid and the efficiency of a computer."[15] Another friend described Stewart as being "as focused as a bullet in flight."[16]

With that efficiency in her work, and her drive to keep moving forward, Martha Stewart has succeeded in achieving an incredible following. In early 1997, a survey indicated there were almost eight million Martha Stewart book and magazine readers, five million television viewers, and sixteen million readers of her "Ask Martha" column, which appears in newspapers across the nation.[17]

Several years ago, before reaching her present-day success, Stewart was asked if she had an ultimate goal. "I just want to have a productive life and be some sort of good legacy," she replied. "I want to teach people. I want to do something good."[18]

It is easy to believe that Martha Stewart will continue "to teach people" and "do something good." In doing so, she will gather even more followers. After all, how many among us can resist "a good thing"?

Chronology

1941—Martha Kostyra born August 3 in Jersey City, New Jersey.

1944—Kostyra family moves to Nutley, New Jersey.

1954—Begins working part-time as a model in television commercials.

1959—Graduates from Nutley High School; awarded full scholarship to New York University; enrolls at Barnard College on a partial scholarship.

1961—Marries Andrew Stewart, July 1.

1964—Receives bachelor of arts degree in European history and architecture, from Barnard College.

1965—Daughter, Alexis, is born, September 27.

1967—Begins working as stockbroker in Wall Street brokerage firm.

1973—Leaves brokerage firm; moves with Andy and Alexis to nineteenth-century farmhouse in Westport, Connecticut; begins restoration of house and garden.

1976—Opens Market Basket, a take-out food shop in Westport.

1977—Closes food shop; begins a catering service.

1978—Establishes catering firm called Martha, Inc.; writes "Quick Cook" column for *House Beautiful*.

1982—First book, *Entertaining* (written with Elizabeth Hawes), is published.

1983—*Martha Stewart's Quick Cook: 200 Easy and Elegant Recipes* is published.

1984—*Martha Stewart's Hors d'Oeuvres: The Creation and Presentation of Fabulous Finger Foods* is published.

1985—*Martha Stewart's Pies and Tarts* is published.

1987—Gives up catering to write books; appears on PBS television special *Holiday Entertaining with Martha Stewart*; begins teaching Entertaining Seminars; *Weddings* (written with Elizabeth Hawes) is published; separates from husband, Andy; signs five-year contract with Kmart Corporation as lifestyle consultant.

1988—*The Wedding Planner* and *Martha Stewart's Quick Cook Menus: Fifty-two Meals You Can Make in Under an Hour* are published; makes a series of videotapes for Crown Video, *Martha Stewart's Secrets of Entertaining*.

1989—*Martha Stewart's Christmas: Entertaining, Decorating, and Giving* is published; makes a series of "Dinner Classics" classical music/menu recordings for CBS Masterworks.

1990—Launches *Martha Stewart Living* magazine, published by Time Warner; divorce from Andy becomes final.

1991—*Martha Stewart's Gardening, Month by Month* is published; Stewart appears twice a month on NBC-TV's *Today* show.

1992—*Martha Stewart's New Old House: Restoration, Renovation, Decoration* is published.

1993—Begins *Martha Stewart Living*, a weekly syndicated television program; *The Best of Martha Stewart Living: Holidays* is published.

1994—Interviews First Lady Hillary Rodham Clinton for NBC-TV's *Today* show; *Menus for Entertaining* and *The Best of Martha Stewart Living: Special Occasions* are published.

1995 —Becomes chairman and chief executive officer of Martha Stewart Living Enterprises, jointly owned by Time Inc. Ventures; appears in prime-time television special on CBS, *Martha Stewart's Home for the Holidays*; *The Martha Stewart Cookbook* and *The Best of Martha Stewart Living: Handmade Christmas* are published.

1996 —Second Christmas special on CBS, *Welcome Home for the Holidays*; *The Best of Martha Stewart Living: Great American Wreaths*, *The Best of Martha Stewart Living: What to Have for Dinner*, and *The Best of Martha Stewart Living: How to Decorate* are published.

1997 —Martha Stewart becomes owner, chairman, and CEO of her new corporation, Martha Stewart Living Omnimedia. *The Best of Martha Stewart Living: Good Things* and *Martha Stewart's Healthy Quick Cook* are published; leaves NBC-TV's *Today* show; appears weekly on CBS-TV's *This Morning* show; launches new daily television program, *Martha Stewart Living Weekdays*; Martha By Mail catalog is published; Martha Stewart Web site makes debut.

Chapter Notes

Chapter 1. A Good Thing

1. Martha Stewart interview, CNN's *Larry King Live*, April 23, 1990, transcript #28, p. 13.

2. Mark Leyner, "Martha Stewart," *Esquire*, August 1995, p. 52.

3. Barbara Lippert, "She's Martha Stewart and You're Not," *New York*, May 15, 1995, cover page.

4. "A Letter From Martha," *Martha Stewart Living*, June 1996, p. 12.

5. Patrick M. Reilly, "Martha Stewart Takes Over Control of Her Empire in Split With Time, Inc.," *The Wall Street Journal*, February 5, 1997, p. B8.

Chapter 2. A Head Start

1. "Martha Stewart," *Current Biography Yearbook*, 1993 (New York: H. W. Wilson, 1993), p. 555.

2. Ibid., p. 556.

3. Martha Stewart, "Putting Down Roots," *Martha Stewart Living*, April 1995, p. 144.

4. Martha Stewart, "Visions of Sugarplums," *Martha Stewart Living*, December 1995–January 1996, p. 156.

5. Jeanie Kasindorf, "Living With Martha," *New York*, January 28, 1991, p. 24.

6. Martha Stewart, "Our Dream Kitchen," *Martha Stewart Living*, September 1996, p. 166.

7. Martha Stewart interview on PBS-TV *Charlie Rose* show, September 15, 1995, transcript #1466, p. 2.

8. Ibid.

9. Elizabeth Sahatjian, "Martha Stewart Entertaining/Decorating Maven." *Cosmopolitan*, August 1990, p. 120.

Chapter 3. Moving On

1. Jeanie Kasindorf, "Living With Martha," *New York*, January 28, 1991, p. 25.

2. Martha Stewart interview on PBS-TV *Charlie Rose* show, September 15, 1995, transcript #1466, p. 2.

3. "Barnard College at a Glance," Office of Public Affairs, Barnard College, New York, N.Y., March 1997.

4. Martha Stewart interview with John Tesh, NBC-TV's *One on One*, September 20, 1991.

5. Michelle Green, "The Best Revenge," *People*, October 2, 1995, p. 106.

6. Kristin McMurran, "Martha Stewart Caters for the Newmans and Redfords, While Andy Cooks Up 'Gnomes,' " *People*, April 14, 1980, p. 106.

7. Ibid., p. 107.

8. Ibid.

9. Martha Stewart, "Remembering," *Martha Stewart Living*, Winter/Spring 1995, p. 272.

10. Martha Stewart, "Of Kitchens and Learning," *Entertaining* (New York: Clarkson N. Potter, 1982), p. 3.

11. Martha Stewart, "The First Harvest," *Martha Stewart Living*, March 1997, p. 184.

12. Martha Stewart, *Martha Stewart's Hors d'Oeuvres: The Creation and Presentation of Fabulous Fingerfoods* (New York: Clarkson N. Potter, 1984), p. 1.

13. Barbara Lippert, "She's Martha Stewart and You're Not," *New York*, May 15, 1995, p. 29.

Chapter 4. A New Direction

1. Kristin McMurran, "Martha Stewart Caters for the Newmans and Redfords, While Andy Cooks Up 'Gnomes,'" *People*, April 14, 1980, p. 106.

2. Martha Stewart interview on PBS-TV *Charlie Rose* show, September 15, 1995, transcript #1466, p. 2.

3. R. Ellen Boddie, "Home-Grown Success," *Working Woman*, December 1980, p. 44.

4. Ibid., p. 47.

5. Martha Stewart, *Entertaining* (New York: Clarkson N. Potter, 1982), p. 6.

6. Jeanie Russell Kasindorf, "Martha, Inc.," *Working Woman*, June 1995, p. 66.

7. McMurran, p. 106.

8. Susan Wood, "The Good Life, Country Style," *House and Garden*, June 1977, p. 96.

9. Boddie, p. 43.

10. Martha Stewart interview with Charlie Rose.

Chapter 5. The Good and the Bad

1. Martha Stewart, speech at National Press Club, Washington, D.C., November 12, 1996, transcript, p. 13.

2. Jeanie Russell Kasindorf, "Martha, Inc.," *Working Woman*, June 1995, p. 31.

3. Martha Stewart interview on PBS-TV *Charlie Rose* show, September 15, 1995, transcript #1466, p. 3.

4. Robin Pogrebin, "Martha Stewart Is Now Master of Her Own Destiny," *The New York Times*, February 8, 1998, sec. 3, p. 14.

5. Jane Anderson, "Entertaining: By Martha Stewart," *Christian Science Monitor*, December 15, 1982, p. 16.

6. Ruth Diebold, "Entertaining: By Martha Stewart," *Library Journal*, December 15, 1982, vol. 107, no. 22, p. 2338.

7. Ruth Diebold, "Martha Stewart's Quick Cook," *Library Journal*, December 15, 1983, p. 2332.

8. Elizabeth L. Bland, "A New Guru of American Taste?" *Time*, December 19, 1988, p. 92.

9. Laura Shapiro, "The Art of Showing Off," *Newsweek*, December 1, 1986, p. 67.

10. Martha Stewart's Holiday Entertaining Seminar, Westport, Conn., November 8, 1988; information courtesy of participant Mary Hecker MacRae.

11. Mary Gillis, "Martha Stewart," *Contemporary Authors* (Detroit: Gale Research, 1997), p. 417.

12. Kim Hubbard and Joyce Seymore, "Martha Stewart, the One-Woman Industry, Adds a New Line for Kmart and Subtracts a Husband," *People*, November 28, 1988, p. 120.

13. Ibid.

14. Jeanie Kasindorf, "Living With Martha," *New York*, January 28, 1991, p. 28.

15. Ibid.

16. Martha Stewart interview with Charlie Rose, p. 5.

17. Elizabeth Sahatjian, "Martha Stewart: Entertaining/Decorating Maven," *Cosmopolitan*, August 1990, p. 120.

18. Hubbard and Seymore, p. 123.

19. Laura Shapiro, "I'm Cooking as Fast as I Can," *Newsweek*, September 4, 1989, p. 63.

20. Jon Etra, "Household Name," *Harper's Bazaar*, May 1990, p. 38.

21. Shapiro, p. 66.

Chapter 6. Growth of a Passion

1. Charles Gandee, "Martha Stewart Talks Turkey," *House and Garden*, May 1990, p. 226.

2. Jeanie Kasindorf, "Living With Martha," *New York*, January 28, 1991, p. 28.

3. Ibid.

4. Martha Stewart, "A Letter From Martha," *Martha Stewart Living*, July/August 1991, p. 4.

5. Patrick M. Reilly, "The Best Revenge," *The Wall Street Journal*, April 10, 1996, p. 1.

6. Jeanie Russell Kasindorf, "Martha, Inc.," *Working Woman*, June 1995, p. 69.

7. Molly Newling, "Martha Stewart: Entertaining/ Decorating Maven," *Cosmopolitan*, August 1990, pp. 120–121.

8. Elizabeth Zeschin, "Martha Stewart's Gardening, Month by Month," *Library Journal*, January 1992, p. 163.

9. Allen Lacy, "Martha Stewart's Gardening, Month by Month," *The New York Times Book Review*, December 1, 1991, p. 43.

10. Curtis Driedger, "Martha Stewart's Gardening, Month by Month," *Quill & Quire*, February 1992, p. 29.

11. Martha Stewart interview, CNN's *Larry King Live*, April 23, 1990, transcript #28, p. 10.

12. Martin Pedersen, "Martha Stewart Cross-Merchandising," *Publishers Weekly*, December 12, 1994, p. 19.

13. Kasindorf, "Martha, Inc.," p. 69.

14. Ibid.

15. Martha Stewart, speech at National Press Club Luncheon, Washington, D.C., November 12, 1996, transcript, p. 4.

16. Cheryl Lavin, "The House of Stewart," *Chicago Tribune*, February 15, 1996, p. 2.

17. Ibid.

Chapter 7. New Ventures

1. Martha Stewart interview, CNN's *Larry King Live*, April 23, 1990, transcript #28, p. 16.

2. Martha Stewart interview of Hillary Rodham Clinton, NBC-TV's *Today*, December 9, 1994, transcript, p. 30.

3. Ibid., p. 31.

4. Martha Stewart interview, CNN's *Larry King Live*, December 5, 1995, transcript #1609, p. 11.

5. Martha Stewart, speech at National Press Club, Washington, D.C., November 12, 1996, transcript, p. 7.

6. "Letters to the Editor," *Martha Stewart Living*, June 1996, p. 26.

7. "Letters to the Editor," *Martha Stewart Living*, July/August 1996, p. 22.

8. "Letters to the Editor," *Martha Stewart Living*, December 1996/January 1997, p. 34.

9. Jeanie Russell Kasindorf, "Martha, Inc.," *Working Woman*, June 1995, p. 28.

10. Ibid.

11. Judith C. Sutton, "The Martha Stewart Cookbook: Collected Recipes for Every Day," *Library Journal*, October 15, 1995, p. 82.

Chapter 8. On the Go

1. "A Letter From Martha," *Martha Stewart Living*, May 1995, p. 10.

2. Martin Pedersen, "Martha Stewart Cross-Merchandising," *Publishers Weekly*, December 12, 1994, p. 19.

3. Ibid.

4. Nancy Bartley, "A Martha Morning: Homing In on the Stewart Way of Living," *The Seattle Times*, May 1, 1997, p. B1.

5. Cheryl Lavin, "The House of Stewart," *Chicago Tribune*, February 15, 1996, p. 1.

6. Patricia McLaughlin, "Public Enemy No. 1," *The New York Times*, November 24, 1996, p. 84.

7. Martha Stewart interview with John Tesh, NBC-TV's *One on One*, September 20, 1991, transcript, p. 5.

8. Benjamin DeMott, "Is Martha Stewart Good for America?" *Lear's*, October 1992, pp. 86–87.

9. "America's 25 Most Influential People," *Time*, June 17, 1996, p. 75.

10. Martha Stewart, speech at National Press Club, Washington, D.C., November 12, 1996, transcript, p. 10.

11. Martha Stewart, *The Best of Martha Stewart Living: Great American Wreaths* (New York: Clarkson N. Potter, 1996), p. 15.

12. Ibid.

Chapter 9. Living—Her Way

1. Jeanie Russell Kasindorf, "Martha, Inc.," *Working Woman*, June 1995, p. 29.

2. Address by Martha Stewart, speech at National Press Club Luncheon, Washington, D.C., November 12, 1996, transcript, p. 13.

3. Michelle Green, "The Best Revenge," *People*, October 2, 1995, p. 106.

4. Martha Stewart interview with John Tesh, NBC-TV's *One on One*, September 20, 1991, transcript, p. 3.

5. Barbara Lippert, "She's Martha Stewart and You're Not," *New York*, May 15, 1995, p. 35.

6. Trish Hall, "Grooming Cats and Dogs," *Martha Stewart Living*, April 1997, pp. 110–116.

7. "Gathering," *The Best of Martha Stewart Living: How to Decorate* (New York: Clarkson N. Potter, 1996), pp. 36–37.

8. Green, p. 110.

9. Beth Landman Keil and Deborah Mitchell, "Intelligencer," *New York*, November 17, 1997, p. 13.

10. Lippert, p. 32.

11. Jeanie Kasindorf, "Living With Martha," *New York,* January 28, 1991, p. 30.

12. Martha Stewart interview, *Oprah,* February 2, 1994.

13. Green, p. 106.

14. "Shortcuts," *Chicago Tribune,* July 27, 1997, sec. 13, p. 6.

15. Martha Stewart interview on *Oprah,* transcript, p. 5.

16. R. Ellen Boddie, "Home-Grown Success," *Working Woman,* December 1980, p. 45.

17. Martha Stewart interview on *Oprah,* transcript, p. 24.

18. Green, p. 110.

19. Martha Stewart interview on PBS-TV *Charlie Rose* show, September 15, 1995, transcript #1466, p. 7.

20. Ibid.

Chapter 10. Riding on Success

1. "America's 25 Most Influential People," *Time,* June 17, 1996, p. 75.

2. Martha Stewart interview with Barbara Walters, ABC-TV, "Ten Most Fascinating People of 1996," December 6, 1996.

3. Martha Stewart interview on PBS-TV *Charlie Rose* show, February 21, 1997, transcript #1841.

4. Patrick M. Reilly, "The Best Revenge, *The Wall Street Journal,* April 10, 1996, p. A1.

5. "Letters to the Editor," *The Wall Street Journal,* May 9, 1996.

6. Patrick M. Reilly, "Martha Stewart Takes Over Control of Her Empire in Split With Time Inc.," *The Wall Street Journal,* February 5, 1997, p. B8.

7. Ibid.

8. Thomas E. Weber, "Watching the Web: A Closer Look," *The Wall Street Journal*, December 22, 1997, p. B5.

9. Interview with Charlie Rose, p. 3.

10. Martha Stewart, "A Letter From Martha," *Martha Stewart Living*, April 1997, p. 12.

11. Gannett News Service, "Stewart Honest About Reasons for Leaving NBC," *Commercial-News* (Danville, Ill.), February 10, 1997, p. 6B.

12. Martha Stewart, "Gathering," in *How to Decorate* (New York: Clarkson N. Potter, 1996), pp. 32–33.

13. Brendan Gill, "Martha's Retreat," *New Yorker*, October 16, 1995, p. 111.

14. James P. Sterba, "Where Martha Stewart's Living," *The Wall Street Journal*, October 16, 1997, p. A20.

15. "The 50 Most Beautiful People in the World 1996," *People*, May 6, 1996, p. 128.

16. Gill, p. 109.

17. Martha Stewart, "A Letter From Martha," *Martha Stewart Living*, December 1996/January 1997, p. 10.

18. Martha Stewart interview with John Tesh, NBC-TV's *One on One*, September 20, 1991, transcript, p. 6.

Further Reading

Collins, Gail. "Martha, Martha." *McCall's*, October 1996, p. 47.

Green, Michelle. "The Best Revenge." *People*, October 2, 1995, p. 100.

Kasindorf, Jeanie. "Living With Martha." *New York*, January 28, 1991, p. 23.

Kasindorf, Jeanie Russell. "Martha, Inc." *Working Woman*, June 1995, p. 26.

Lippert, Barbara. "She's Martha Stewart and You're Not." *New York*, May 15, 1995, p. 26.

Wooten, Sara M. *Martha Stewart*. Woodbridge, Conn: Blackbirch Press, 1998.

Zaslow, Jeffrey. "Straight Talk: Martha Stewart." *USA Weekend*, December 6–8, 1996, p. 14.

On the Internet

The official Web site
<http://www.marthastewart.com>

The unofficial Martha Stewart Web site
<http://www.du.edu/~szerobni/>

Index